YES! SUCCESS!
Discovering God's
Amazing Plan For You

Dan Hurst

Living Power
Publishing

www.LivingPower.com
(660) 851-1510

ISBN: 0692323147
ISBN 13: 9780692323144

Excellent and to the point. While I have enjoyed the previous book I read of yours, this one I think has a much larger audience. I can see it as an additional reading for "leadership courses." I really found nothing to criticize and lots to appreciate.

Richard Hastings,
President and CEO of Saint Luke's Health
System, Retired

In this book by Dan Hurst you'll discover how "His" strategy, "His" ways and "His" purpose are key elements to your success. The "His" is not Dan's, it's God's. Dan Hurst is the messenger who delivers it masterfully, clearly and with honesty. Read this book and reach the greatest success you could ever imagine.

David Naster
Author and Producer of TV series: "You Just
Have To Laugh"

A key book that will surely be inspirational to people in all walks of life. Dan's ability to tie together life experiences and insights with Biblical principles is awesome!

Julie Sherriff, President
Sherriff & Associates, Inc.

For many years I was made to feel guilty by certain people about the success of my business. I struggled with this immensely, even to the point of wondering if I was doing what God had directed me to do. Dan really brings home the point of being in God's plan and understanding that when we are able to accept that, the blessings that we receive from our successes can and should be shared with others. Knowing you are doing God's will is a success story in itself.

Bob Perkins,
Founder of Nature's Pantry

ACKNOWLEDGMENTS

God has so richly blessed my life with people who have influenced me beyond what they will ever know. From Virgilio Silva, the humble woodworker in Honduras who taught me that life is music; to Dr. Otis and Marge Hill in South Carolina, who taught me by example that people are worth loving and caring for; to my church family at First Baptist Church, Raytown, who taught me that as brothers and sisters in Christ we are family, no matter what.

I'm also very grateful for my editors, Angie Kiesling and Charles Joyner, they are such a blessing. And for my friends that took the time to review the book and comment on it, I am thankful beyond words!

But especially I'm grateful for my sons Eric, Jared, and Jordan, who give me a reason every day to get up and do it again. I don't mean to just get up and go to work. I mean to get up and be a father who loves their mother and seeks to be the best father I can be to them. They continue to be a motivation for whatever success I enjoy. I am so very proud of them.

1 My son, do not forget my teaching, but let your heart keep my commandments,

2 for length of days and years of life and peace they will add to you.

3 Let not steadfast love and faithfulness forsake you; bind them around your neck; write them on the tablet of your heart.

4 So you will find favor and good success in the sight of God and man.

Proverbs 3:1-4 (ESV)

TABLE OF CONTENTS

FOREWORD

I'm delighted that my friend Dan Hurst has penned this volume on Biblical principles for success. Our power-hungry, work-driven American culture desperately needs to hear a word from God on this topic. It's easy for us to get caught up in the temptation to believe that material success is the *source* of achieving the "life of our dreams." Success matters, but how you *chase* it matters even more.

Dan Hurst does an excellent job of showing us that our primary purpose is in our Creator, not our career – so we must live and work for our Creator first. If you truly take to heart the message contained in this book – it will transform how you look at life.

What exactly is success? Simply stated, success is progressing in the will of God. John Maxwell defines success as having three dimensions – "Knowing your purpose in life, growing to your maximum potential, and sowing seeds to benefit others." I am convinced that you need a dream that is destined to fail without divine intervention because it will force you to get on your knees and seek the face of God. Big dreams are the best thing for us spiritually. They make us pray. They make us seek after Him with our whole heart. They force us to live the way we ought to live—in complete dependence on God.

Have you ever asked someone, "What is your number one ambition in life?" and had them say to you, "I want to be a massive failure!" Of course not. Everybody wants to be successful. No matter what you do—nobody sets out in life hoping to be a failure. So you will be encouraged to know that the Bible talks a great deal about success. God is highly interested in your success and He wants you to be successful – but He wants you to achieve that success *His* way. Our culture has taught us that success is tied to two things: Education (what you know) and Connections (who you know). Of course both of those are good – but God says that the secret to true and lasting success is tied to how we receive and respond to the teachings of God's Word. God told Joshua, *"This Book of the Law shall not depart from your mouth, but you shall meditate in it day and night, that you may observe to do all that is written in it. For then you will make your way prosperous, and then you will have good success."* When you have the

presence of God guarding you and the principles of God guiding you – the end result will be
your fulfillment of His purpose and plan for you.
So in essence, success simply means finding out
what God wants you to "be and do" and giving
your best to "being it and doing it!"

I once heard about a book which had a title that
intrigued me. It was entitled *Turtle on a Fencepost*. The premise of the book is that if you ever
see a turtle on a fencepost, you can rest assured
that he did not get there on his own. Someone or
something else had placed it on that platform. One
of my favorite Hebrew words is *Ebenezer* which
means "hitherto the Lord has helped me." When
you take the next step on the path towards fulfill-
ing the goals that God has laid on your heart – it
is an Ebenezer moment. May this book serve as a
catalyst for God stirring your heart and desiring
more for that which only He can bring to pass in
your life.

In the classic movie *Ben Hur*, there is a scene
where they are in the chariot races. The problem behind the scenes though was that Charlton
Heston was having trouble driving his chariot.
They couldn't get a body double to do the part
because they needed close-up camera shots of
Heston. However, he felt that he just couldn't do
it. He couldn't pull it off driving the chariot in
such a way to make it look like he was winning
the race. Finally he went to the director, William

Wyler and said, "Mr. Wyler, I can't win this race! The script says I have to win, but I'm having too hard of a time just keeping up!"

The director gave a response that Charlton Heston said he would never forget. Wyler replied, "Your job is not to succeed, your job is to stay in the chariot! I'll make sure you succeed."

My friend, when you live in God's presence, obey His principles, and fulfill His purpose for your life – you will win in this race towards success!

Dr. Brandon S. Park
Pastor of First Baptist Raytown, Missouri

PREFACE

I am not so much proud of this book as I am burdened by it.

For many years it has been my contention that all the answers we need for life can be found in the Word of God. I still believe that. However, discovering and sharing the practical truths of God's Word is a heavy responsibility that I don't take lightly.

I am not a success guru. I'm just a small businessman trying to follow God's principles both for my life and my business. This book is a compilation of those discoveries that I seek to apply every day.

When you are finished reading this book, start over. Keep reading these principles until they become a regular part of your life. You will never be the same. I know. I speak from experience.

True direction and affirmation come from the Holy Spirit. I trust Him to confirm His truths here. That's what I've attempted to do in this book – just share the basic principles and let the Holy Spirit apply them to your life. No doubt each individual reader will draw different conclusions and realizations from this.

There are a few key thoughts in this book that you will find in some form in some of my other books. Many principles cross over into different areas and subjects. I apologize if it seems like repetition, but they are integral to the principles of success as much as they are to other key principles for life.

These principles work. They are not mine; they are right from the Word of God. I seek to apply them to my life and my business and have found them to be trustworthy. God has given me the privilege of sharing these around the world, and the reports are the same: they work.

INTRODUCTION

What? Another book about finding success?

Sort of.

Several years ago I lost my job. Well, I didn't really lose it. It was taken away from me by a rather cruel and unprincipled boss who claimed to be a Christian. Within a few months, I lost almost everything of financial value in my life, including my home. It was a very dark time in my life.

I remember vividly how my wife Marcia and I gathered our three small boys around us and explained to them that I was no longer employed and that things would be very different for a while until I could find another job. That "while" lasted ten months.

We had the great fortune (or rather godly intervention) of having been taught by a man who walks with God: Dr. Lew Miller, a pastor/friend of ours. Lew had taught us the biblical principles upon which we based our marriage as newlyweds. As we started our family, we built upon that foundation, which included financial truths in addition to keys for a strong marriage and solid parenting. Those ten months without a job were really nothing more than a chapter exam in our lives.

I made a commitment to my wife and boys and myself on that cold, gray November morning that we would stay true to biblical principles when dealing with each problem and crisis. I figured that if the power that raised Jesus from the grave was living in me, He could solve my menial problems.

For the next several months, when not out beating the streets looking for a job, I spent time in the Word of God. I believed, and still do, that when Jesus said He had come to bring us "life abundant" (John 10:10), that meant we are to get the most out of life – personal, business, social, etc.

So it all started with discovering what the Bible has to say about success and how one achieves it. I quickly realized that my goals and strategies for success were quite misguided.

Over the next several years I learned to apply these biblical principles in my life. A few years ago it happened again. I was let go from my job after many years. However this time I had learned my lesson. For a few years I had been building a second business, knowing the day would come when it would be my main business. That was nothing but the leading of God.

In that process of building a business, these truths changed my life. I trust they will do no less for you.

I grew up on the mission field, the son of missionary parents in Honduras. One of the most successful men I have ever known is Virgilio Silva, a humble woodworker in the capital city of Tegucigalpa. He had everything he needed and wanted. He was happy. He loved to sit out on the veranda of his tiny wooden shack and play his guitar.

He taught me to play the guitar. One of my favorite memories of him is how he would show me certain chords and say, "Music is like life. Play the notes you want and don't worry about stopping or fighting the others. Sometimes you'll play the wrong note, but the way to fix that is by finding and playing the right note."

But then he said something really interesting. "The secret to good music is the next note. Make each note a step to the next note."

Years later, that principle became life-changing.

Personal goal setting and success have gotten a bad rap among Christians. Somewhere between the freedom of Calvinism and the responsibility of Arminianism lies the crucial process of setting valid personal goals—goals that fulfill both our freedom and responsibility.

A fatalistic mindset that operates under the delusion that we have no real control over life and must accept whatever comes our way is contrary to what God tells us in His Word. In fact, God has quite a bit to say about success and setting personal goals.

We're taught in this world that success is the "prize" for overcoming the odds and obstacles of whatever we're pursuing—even if those roadblocks are people. Nothing could be further from the truth.

The Bible gives us some very clear principles for success and setting goals. If God gave us so much in His Word about this, we should pay attention!

This is a book about developing success and goals.

Yes, another one. However, this book isn't so much a "how to" book as much as it is "why" success happens.

Also, this book is the result of a personal quest.

God has blessed me immensely. This book imparts what I'm learning as God has taken me through this wonderful journey of discovering His way of doing things.

I'm here to tell you that God's ways work. For the past several years I've been applying these biblical principles to my life. They are life-changing. They are soul-surprising. They are often mind-boggling. But the bottom line is they work.

This book is intentionally short. After I designed the outline for it, I realized I had two options. I could fill the book with examples and commentary to make it longer, or I could keep it shorter and just deal with the "meat and potatoes." I chose the latter.

My hope is that because the book is short you will read it over and over. As you do, draw your own conclusions and develop the principles herein according to your own experience. A writer couldn't ask for more.

CHAPTER 1

WHAT IS SUCCESS?

We are overrun with plans and devices for success. The world is full of them. Check out a bookstore's self-help section. Or do a Web search on the word "success." At the time I was writing this book, I found almost *one billion* Web matches! Frankly, the vast majority of comments and advice I found was appalling. In fact, most of the information was downright misleading and misguided.

We are obsessed with success. Why?

Perhaps it's because we are surrounded by such lack of success. Perhaps it is because we know how fragile success is and how difficult it is to attain and maintain.

It seems that everybody has a unique plan to succeed. The Bible says there is only one plan that leads to real success: God's plan. In fact, God's plan is such a sure thing that we should see it the way He does. It's not a theory. Not a method. Not a formula. It's a command.

The Bible says there is only one plan that leads to real success: God's plan. In fact, God's plan is such a sure thing that we should see it the way He does. It's not a theory. Not a method. Not a formula. It's a command.

The truth is that God wants you to be successful. He wants it so much that He has mandated
it, as you will discover in His Word.

> *Commit to the LORD whatever you do, and
> your plans will succeed.*
>
> Proverbs 16:3

It's His desire that you be successful! That
means failing to be successful is to fail God's desire for you. That is nothing less than sin.

Think about that. To fail at being successful according to God's plan is sin. What happens when
we sin? We're separated from God. When you are
separated from God you cannot know all that He
has for you.

Separation from God's will is the greatest failure of all. No other failure even comes close to
that horrific condition. Often such failure leads
to other failures and losses. It becomes a vicious
cycle.

The Bible encourages success to the point that
we are told to plan ahead for it:

> *...those who plan what is good find love
> and faithfulness.*
>
> Proverbs 14:22

There is a dangerous attitude within the Christian community that success is worldly and

therefore wrong, or at least questionable. Granted, the world's concept of success is often terribly self-centered and brutal—even cruel—but that is not real success. True success is anything but worldly.

Before we define success, let's consider the differences between how man and God perceive success.

Man's Success

Ask any number of people on the street how success happens and you'll hear four things over and over:

1. A lot of hard work
2. A lot of time
3. A good investment
4. A little luck

A little luck? What's that? Does that mean a fleeting chance? The vague possibility that things will go right? Does it mean that the right circumstances happen to line up just right? Or that the positive energy outweighs the negative energy?

Success is no more being fortunate than a horse is just a lucky donkey.

We tend to think that success and the pursuit of it is an invention of man. The result is that we define it by worldly concepts. We assume that our success is dependent on us. It's the old "if it is to be, it's up to me" syndrome.

There was an old football coach who loved to throw such clichés around. He had them on posters all over the locker room. He quoted them in his pep talks. He shouted them from the sidelines. One day one of his receivers, totally frustrated with the way things were going, shouted back, "Coach, I know if it is to be, it's up to me, but if you want me to score, gimme the ball more!"

I know exactly how that young man felt. Success-driven people have great confidence in themselves and sometimes think that in order to succeed all they need is a chance; all they need is the right opportunity.

The fact is that success is not simply "up to me." Far too many extenuating circumstances determine success for it to be entirely up to you.

Furthermore, if success were entirely up to you, it would be limited because man's view of success is based on limiting factors such as perception, concept, and valuation.

Man's perception of success is limited to his experience. He sees success as either something he has achieved or something he has not. Even then his perception of success is colored by his concept of what it is. Man's concept of success is influenced by what other people have defined or valued as success. So man often sets his own standards of success, never knowing how valid they are.

Then man really complicates matters by setting a valuation on success. Value is a relative matter. What may be of great value to one person may be insignificant to another. But if one puts a valuation on success, he has determined that one of the marks of his success will be what others have defined as valuable.

In other words, if a person decides that one of the marks of success is an expensive car he has allowed a cultural influence to define his success. But if that person has not achieved his true potential, or even finished what he set out to accomplish, how can one consider him successful even if he drives an expensive car?

Man's general concept of success is misdirected and limited.

One of the key principles of man's concept of success is that it requires scheming. Scheming is seeking personal benefit regardless of the cost to others.

> *This only have I found: God made mankind upright [originally], but men have gone in search of many schemes.*
>
> Ecclesiastes 7:29

> *Be still before the LORD and wait patiently for him; do not fret when men succeed in their ways, when they carry out their wicked schemes.*
>
> Psalm 37:7

> *Those who devise wicked schemes are near, but they are far from your law.*
>
> Psalm 119:150

Beware of any plan, yours or others, that seeks personal benefit without regard for the cost to others. Any plan that benefits you because it takes from others without returning an equal or better value is a scheme. It's off-limits for the Christian.

Man's concept of success results in arrogance and pride.

> *In his arrogance the wicked man hunts down the weak, who are caught in the schemes he devises.*
>
> Psalm 10:2

Years ago I briefly worked for a company that sold photography plans. I didn't know it when I took the job, but I quickly discovered that their lead-generation method was, at best, deceptive. The company would send out direct-mail pieces that told people they had won a TV or some other nice prize. All they had to do was come down to the office to claim their winnings. When they got there, they had to select a number off a board. The number would correspond to the prize they had won. Almost all the numbers corresponded to some rather cheap prizes.

Once they chose their number, the couple was told they could trade it in and have the prize of their choice if they purchased the photography plan.

I was bothered by the sleazy approach the company used. When I asked the boss why they used that method to get people in the door, he responded, "Because the world is full of sucker fish, and we're just reeling them in."

I quit.

Not before I accidentally gave away two television sets.

One of the natural byproducts of man's success is pride. Oh, it may be suppressed by feigned humbleness, but generally a person who has achieved success by his own methods will be arrogantly protective of his accomplishments.

He can't help it. Believing in his plan is what got him there. He has proven, in his own mind, that his method works. He has the goods to prove it.

The psalmist noticed the same thing:

...do not grant the wicked their desires, O LORD; do not let their plans succeed, or they will become proud.

Psalm 140:8

Such pride is directly in conflict with God's ways. In fact, God's success leads to great humbleness because one realizes that success comes not by one's own effort but by the will of God.

Man's success is never a given.

Perhaps one of the reasons man becomes so arrogantly protective of his own success is because he knows how easy it would be to lose it. He knows how fragile his success is.

Human success is often limited and therefore essentially controlled by unforeseen and uncontrollable circumstances. How many stories have you heard about someone building a successful business only to lose it all to a natural disaster or a national economic downturn? Even more heartbreaking are the stories of those who never achieve any sort of success in spite of all their work and then eventually lose what little they had accomplished.

However, there is no more disturbing story than that of one who achieves success at the expense of innocent people. Isaiah refers to that type of person—the man or woman who seeks success at any cost.

> *10 You have trusted in your wickedness and have said, 'No one sees me.' Your wisdom and knowledge mislead you when you say to yourself, 'I am, and there is none besides me.'*
> *11 Disaster will come upon you, and you will not know how to conjure it away. A calamity will fall upon you that you cannot ward off with a ransom; a catastrophe you cannot foresee will suddenly come upon you.*
> *12 "Keep on, then, with your magic spells and with your many sorceries, which you have labored at since childhood. Perhaps you will succeed, perhaps you will cause terror.*
>
> Isaiah 47:10-12

Let me give a warning here to those who follow business strategies and plans that are based on ungodly principles. You may achieve your version of success, but it has eternal consequences. Such methods leave a wake of disaster, calamity, and catastrophe.

We've seen that sort of thing with the massive failures of several international corporations. But those same disastrous principles also apply to small business practices. Be careful that you do not fall into that trap.

I don't want to condemn the people who have achieved their goals and dreams by their own legitimate methods. Many of the success plans and patterns I've studied and read about seem to have their roots in biblical principles. But man's success will never be greater than God's.

> *Many are the plans in a man's heart, but it is the LORD's purpose that prevails.*
>   Proverbs 19:21

> *There is no wisdom, no insight, no plan that can succeed against the LORD.*
>   Proverbs 21:30

It is important to point out that sometimes God allows man's plans to succeed in order to accomplish His purposes. Take Nebuchadnezzar for example. He was a powerful king of Babylon, intent on furthering his kingdom. He was not in any way interested in serving the God of the Jews, but God refers to him through the prophet Jeremiah as His servant and declares that He will use him to accomplish His purpose.

> *9 I will summon all the peoples of the north and my servant Nebuchadnezzar king of Babylon," declares the LORD, "and I will*

> *bring them against this land and its in-*
> *habitants and against all the surround-*
> *ing nations. I will completely destroy*
> *them and make them an object of horror*
> *and scorn, and an everlasting ruin.*
> *10 I will banish from them the sounds of*
> *joy and gladness, the voices of bride and*
> *bridegroom, the sound of millstones and*
> *the light of the lamp.*
> *11 This whole country will become a des-*
> *olate wasteland, and these nations will*
> *serve the king of Babylon seventy years.*
>
> Jeremiah 25:9-11

Now why would God do such a thing? The answer is found in the history recorded in the Old
Testament:

> *14 Furthermore, all the leaders of the*
> *priests and the people became more and*
> *more unfaithful, following all the detest-*
> *able practices of the nations and defiling*
> *the temple of the LORD, which he had con-*
> *secrated in Jerusalem.*
> *15 The LORD, the God of their ancestors,*
> *sent word to them through his messengers*
> *again and again, because he had pity on his*
> *people and on his dwelling place.*

16 But they mocked God's messengers, despised his words and scoffed at his prophets until the wrath of the LORD was aroused against his people and there was no remedy. 17 He brought up against them the king of the Babylonians, who killed their young men with the sword in the sanctuary, and did not spare young men or young women, the elderly or the infirm. God gave them all into the hands of Nebuchadnezzar.

2 Chronicles 36:14-17

So God allowed Nebuchadnezzar's success to accomplish His purpose, which was to bring His people back to Himself.

Interestingly, we read in Daniel that Nebuchadnezzar had his own confrontation with God:

34 At the end of that time, I, Nebuchadnezzar, raised my eyes toward heaven, and my sanity was restored. Then I praised the Most High; I honored and glorified him who lives forever. His dominion is an eternal dominion; his kingdom endures from generation to generation.
35 All the peoples of the earth are regarded as nothing. He does as he pleases with the powers of heaven and the peoples of the

earth. No one can hold back his hand or say to him: "What have you done?"

36 At the same time that my sanity was restored, my honor and splendor were returned to me for the glory of my kingdom. My advisers and nobles sought me out, and I was restored to my throne and became even greater than before.

37 Now I, Nebuchadnezzar, praise and exalt and glorify the King of heaven, because everything he does is right and all his ways are just. And those who walk in pride he is able to humble.

Daniel 4:34-37

You've no doubt heard countless other stories of people who have achieved stature, wealth, and fame only to become disillusioned with it all before turning to God.

I had a very dear friend who for security reasons must remain anonymous. He climbed the ladder of "success" in organized crime. He had it all going for him as far as he was concerned—money, possessions, glamour, and certainly an exciting life.

Life was good until one day while he was casually talking with a man he'd been contracted to kill, the man said offhandedly, "You know, I look around at all the stuff we've got, and I wonder what's the point. I mean, do you ever wonder what's the purpose of life? I ain't got no purpose. You got a purpose?"

That simple question set my friend on a quest. For some reason, he started slipping into the Sunday morning services at the little church where I was serving. He would come in after the service started, sit in the back, and leave before the service was over.

I noticed him, and after a few Sundays I found myself burdened for him. I'd never met him, but I felt that gentle push from God telling me I needed to connect with this guy.

The next Sunday I watched for him. Sure enough, he slipped into the service late. A few minutes before the service was over, as he slipped out the door, I stepped out a different door and met him in the corridor.

I said, "Hi. I'm glad I finally caught you."

He was stunned. He just looked at me, not knowing what to do or say. Apparently that's not something a person in organized crime wants to hear.

I asked him if he had time for a cup of coffee. He did. And that was the beginning of a most unusual friendship.

Slowly, after a few coffee breaks and a few lunches, he began asking the questions buried deep inside him:

"Is there a purpose to life?"

"Does God really care?"

"How can I know God's purpose for me?"

"Does God still have a plan for my life?"

It wasn't long before he decided that he needed to turn his life over to God and follow His purpose and plan for his life. He opened up and told me who he was and what his life was. I had started to suspect that already, but he confirmed it.

In the process of telling me about his life he said, "I realized I had everything I wanted but nothing that I needed."

Here was a man who literally carried thousands of dollars in cash in his pocket, owned several restaurants, sent his kids to private school, and owned expensive houses and cars, and yet he realized that his life would be unfulfilled and unsuccessful until he turned control of it over to God.

Man's concept of success is too shortsighted. True success is bigger than man, and it reaches far beyond man's comprehension. It accomplishes far more than man can dream. Real success is not limited by man's talents and abilities. It finds its roots in time past and leaves its indelible mark on man's future. True success has eternal implications.

True success is not what man accomplishes, but what God does. God's concept of success is far greater! In fact, man's concept of success is an embarrassment compared to God's.

Sow your seed in the morning, and at evening let not your hands be idle, for you do

*not know which will succeed, whether this
or that, or whether both will do equally well.*
                                    Ecclesiastes 11:6

Let's look at nine principles of God's concept of success.

1) Success is always about meeting needs.

That simple statement will revolutionize your concept of success. Success is not about wants. It's about needs. It doesn't matter if you're starting your first job mowing lawns or well on your way to building a huge conglomerate. Success is about meeting needs.

This one simple concept is the reason so many companies fail. The minute a business decision is made based on want—especially personal want—instead of meeting needs, that's the moment the company starts to fail.

Look at all the major corporations that have had such disastrous demises and you will find key decisions made on the basis of want—technically, greed. They sabotaged themselves because they forgot this one simple truth and destroyed themselves and a lot of innocent people.

Success is about
meeting needs.

Notice the servant's key motivation in this passage from Genesis 24. He sought to meet a need.

> *10 Then the servant left, taking with him ten of his master's camels loaded with all kinds of good things from his master. He set out for Aram Naharaim and made his way to the town of Nahor.*
>
> *11 He had the camels kneel down near the well outside the town; it was toward evening, the time the women go out to draw water.*
>
> *12 Then he prayed, "LORD, God of my master Abraham, make me <u>successful</u> today, and show kindness to my master Abraham. 13 See, I am standing beside this spring, and the daughters of the townspeople are coming out to draw water.*
>
> *14 May it be that when I say to a young woman, 'Please let down your jar that I may have a drink,' and she says, 'Drink, and I'll water your camels too' —let her be the one you have chosen for your servant Isaac. By this I will know that you have shown kindness to my master."*
>
> *15 Before he had finished praying, Rebekah came out with her jar on her shoulder. She was the daughter of Bethuel son of Milkah, who was the wife of Abraham's brother Nahor.*

16 The woman was very beautiful, a virgin; no man had ever slept with her. She went down to the spring, filled her jar and came up again.

17 The servant hurried to meet her and said, "Please give me a little water from your jar."

18 "Drink, my lord," she said, and quickly lowered the jar to her hands and gave him a drink.

19 After she had given him a drink, she said, "I'll draw water for your camels too, until they have had enough to drink."

20 So she quickly emptied her jar into the trough, ran back to the well to draw more water, and drew enough for all his camels.

21 Without saying a word, the man watched her closely to learn whether or not the LORD had made his journey successful.

22 When the camels had finished drinking, the man took out a gold nose ring weighing a beka and two gold bracelets weighing ten shekels.

23 Then he asked, "Whose daughter are you? Please tell me, is there room in your father's house for us to spend the night?"

24 She answered him, "I am the daughter of Bethuel, the son that Milkah bore to Nahor."

25 And she added, "We have plenty of straw and fodder, as well as room for you to spend the night."

26 Then the man bowed down and worshiped the LORD...

34 So he said, "I am Abraham's servant.

35 The LORD has blessed my master abundantly, and he has become wealthy. He has given him sheep and cattle, silver and gold, male and female servants, and camels and donkeys.

36 My master's wife Sarah has borne him a son in her old age, and he has given him everything he owns.

37 And my master made me swear an oath, and said, 'You must not get a wife for my son from the daughters of the Canaanites, in whose land I live,

38 but go to my father's family and to my own clan, and get a wife for my son.'

39 "Then I asked my master, 'What if the woman will not come back with me?'

40 "He replied, 'The LORD, before whom I have walked faithfully, will send his angel with you and make your journey a success, so that you can get a wife for my son from my own clan and from my father's family.

41 You will be released from my oath if, when you go to my clan, they refuse to give her to you—then you will be released from my oath.'

42 "When I came to the spring today, I said, 'LORD, God of my master Abraham, if you

*will, please grant <u>success</u> to the journey on
which I have come.*
*43 See, I am standing beside this spring.
If a young woman comes out to draw water and I say to her, "Please let me drink a
little water from your jar,"*
*44 and if she says to me, "Drink, and I'll draw
water for your camels too," let her be the one
the LORD has chosen for my master's son.'*
*45 "Before I finished praying in my heart,
Rebekah came out, with her jar on her
shoulder. She went down to the spring and
drew water, and I said to her, 'Please give
me a drink.'*
*46 "She quickly lowered her jar from her
shoulder and said, 'Drink, and I'll water
your camels too.' So I drank, and she wa-
tered the camels also.*

Genesis 24:10-46 (emphasis added)

This is a major key to success. I call it the Principle of Need. It is fundamental to the way God
operates. He seeks to meet needs. Everything
God does is centered on meeting needs.

*And my God will meet all your needs accord-
ing to his glorious riches in Christ Jesus.*

Philippians 4:19

Check it out. I challenge you to find one example in the Bible where God wasn't trying to meet some need. Simply put, this is the way God works. He is in the business of meeting needs.

Therefore, it just makes sense to embrace this key principle for success. Success is always focused on meeting needs.

2) Success is an act of God.

There is no clearer evidence of this in the Bible than the story of Joseph.

> *2 The LORD was with Joseph, and he became a successful man, and he was in the house of his Egyptian master.*
> *3 His master saw that the LORD was with him and that the LORD caused all that he did to succeed in his hands.*
>
> Genesis 39:2-3(ESV)

> *The warden paid no attention to anything under Joseph's care, because the LORD was with Joseph and gave him success in whatever he did.*
>
> Genesis 39:23

Arrogance and true success are mutually exclusive. In fact, success and humility go hand-in-hand. How so? Because success is an act of God. The individual who is truly successful understands that his success is not because of anything he has done, but rather what God has done. It's all God. The focus, the glory, and the honor all go to God, not the individual. That is true humility.

3) Success is the result of the presence of God.

The secret of David's success was that God was at work in and through his life.

> *12 Saul was afraid of David, because the LORD was with David but had departed from Saul.*
> *13 So he sent David away from him and gave him command over a thousand men, and David led the troops in their campaigns.*
> *14 In everything he did he had great success, because the LORD was with him.*
>
> 1 Samuel 18:12-14

The very nature of God is success. Anything that God touches is naturally successful—by His standards. So wherever God is, success reigns.

Sin, on the other hand, is the gateway to failure. Sin is that which is contrary to the nature of God. Sin cannot exist in the presence of God because of His purity.

Think of it this way: if you have a perfectly sterile glass of water and put just one grain of dirt in the glass, the water is no longer sterile. That's the way it is with God. His presence is perfect. Sin cannot enter His presence. Otherwise it would destroy the purity and perfection of God's presence. God simply will not allow it into His presence. That's why it is so important that the one who seeks to commune with God confesses sin and claims forgiveness before enjoying the presence of God.

One who enjoys and lives in the presence of God will also know the success that His nature produces.

Success is not about what you do. It's about what God does.

4) Success is the result of God fulfilling His promises.

This is the key part of David's success.

> *30 When the LORD has fulfilled for my lord every good thing he promised*

*concerning him and has appointed him
ruler over Israel,
31 my lord will not have on his con-
science the staggering burden of need-
less bloodshed or of having avenged
himself. And when the LORD your God
has brought my lord success, remember
your servant."*

1 Samuel 25:30-31

This is an exciting realization. God has promised success to His children. The apostle Paul re-
affirmed this promise:

*If you belong to Christ, then you are
Abraham's seed, and heirs according to
the promise." You are an heir to all that
God has to offer.*

Galatians 3:29

Now, to receive an inheritance, normally
the giver must pass away. Well, that's exactly what happened when Christ died on the
cross. Jesus died on the cross for you and your
inheritance was made available to you at that
moment – even before you were born! The promised inheritance has been issued to you. You
simply have to claim it according to the instructions.

5) Success is the result of obedience to God.

Read that statement again!

If anyone learned this powerful truth, it was Moses. So much so that he warned the Israelites about the danger of disobedience.

> *38 Of the men who went to explore the land, only Joshua son of Nun and Caleb son of Jephunneh survived.*
>
> *39 When Moses reported this to all the Israelites, they mourned bitterly.*
>
> *40 Early the next morning they set out for the highest point in the hill country, saying, "Now we are ready to go up to the land the LORD promised. Surely we have sinned!"*
>
> *41 But Moses said, "Why are you disobeying the LORD'S command? This will not succeed!*
>
> *42 Do not go up, because the LORD is not with you. You will be defeated by your enemies,*
>
> *43 for the Amalekites and the Canaanites will face you there. Because you have turned away from the LORD, he will not be with you and you will fall by the sword."*
>
> Numbers 14:38-43

David also learned how important obedience is to success. He made a fascinating statement to his son Solomon.

> *11 "Now, my son, the LORD be with you, and may you have success and build the house of the LORD your God, as he said you would.*
> *12 May the LORD give you discretion and understanding when he puts you in command over Israel, so that you may keep the law of the LORD your God.*
> *13 Then you will have success if you are careful to observe the decrees and laws that the LORD gave Moses for Israel. Be strong and courageous. Do not be afraid or discouraged.*
>
> 1 Chronicles 22:11-13

David made it very clear to Solomon that success was directly related to obedience to God. It isn't about following a formula. It isn't about wise investing. It isn't about working hard. It's about obeying God.

This seems like such a simple principle, but it is a critical one.

Obedience opens the doors for God's blessing. However, disobedience closes the doors to God's blessing. God simply will not bless those who are disobedient to Him. That's true for individuals, for families, for businesses, even for churches.

It's not that God doesn't want to bless you. It's just that He won't—if you're disobedient. He's not going to bless or condone disobedience or any other sin.

6) Success is an act of faith.

I love that statement. It is one of the most rewarding things I have ever discovered.

The concept of faith is one of the most misunderstood issues in the Christian life. Most people would define faith as believing in something. For example, if you have faith you will not have anything bad happen to you, or you will overcome some difficulty, or you will become successful in some arena.

For some people, faith is a way of manipulating God.

That's not what faith is at all. By its Greek definition and concept, faith is trusting obedience to the known will of God.

That's it.

Look at Hebrews 11. In every case where someone was considered a person of faith, they already knew what God wanted and simply obeyed.

Faith is acting on what you know God wants.

Faith is trusting obedience to the known will of God.

Faith can't manipulate or will success. It can't. It's not about that. Remember, success is something God does, not what you do.

This is a crucial point. Notice the importance of it in the words of Jehoshaphat:

> *Early in the morning they left for the Desert of Tekoa. As they set out, Jehoshaphat stood and said, "Listen to me, Judah and people of Jerusalem! Have faith in the LORD your God and you will be upheld; have faith in his prophets and you will be successful."*
>
> Chronicles 20:20

This is a fascinating statement. The instruction is very clear: faith in God leads to success. Once we understand this simple yet dynamic truth, we can begin to understand how success is an act of faith – trusting obedience to the known will of God.

7) Success is the result of right priorities.

> *3 Uzziah was sixteen years old when he became king, and he reigned in Jerusalem fifty-two years. His mother's name was Jekoliah; she was from Jerusalem.*

4 He did what was right in the eyes of the LORD, just as his father Amaziah had done.
5 He sought God during the days of Zechariah, who instructed him in the fear of God. As long as he sought the LORD, God gave him success.

2 Chronicles 26:3-5

Notice Uzziah's priorities: 1) to do what was right in the eyes of God, which he learned from his father; 2) to know God; and 3) to receive spiritual instruction from God's messenger. The result was God-given success.

Now, from the world's standpoint, he was successful without doing those things. He was after all the king. How much more successful could one be? But he had a higher ideal—to be successful in God's eyes, by God's standards. So his priorities measured up to that higher standard.

Right priorities are only right by your standard of success. Whatever you consider to be "success" will define your priorities.

I know a man who is a business consultant. He teaches corporations how to succeed. He's good at it. But his personal life is in shambles. He knows the theories of success, but that's all they are to him: theories.

His personal priorities are far different from what he teaches. His personal standard of

success is far lower than the theories he es-
pouses. Not that he doesn't want things to be
different in his personal life. He does. We've
talked about it often. But he's not willing to
make the personal commitment to a higher
standard of success, and so his priorities stay
at the level of his standard.

Show me your true priorities and I'll show you
your standard of success. Your priorities reveal
your standard of success.

8) True success always glorifies God.

This principle alone defines as abject failures so
many people and companies that are successful
by the world's standards. So many people who
chase the false and elusive concepts of success
that the world teaches miss out on the spiritual
value of success.

The psalmist equates success with a focus on
God.

> *1 May the LORD answer you when you are
> in distress; may the name of the God of Ja-
> cob protect you.*
> *2 May he send you help from the sanctuary
> and grant you support from Zion.*
> *3 May he remember all your sacrifices and
> accept your burnt offerings.*

*4 May he give you the desire of your heart
and make all your plans succeed.
5 May we shout for joy over your victory
and lift up our banners in the name of
our God. May the LORD grant all your
requests.*

Psalm 20:1-5

There is an interesting correlation in the Bible
between true success and godly worship. Success
is the result of focus on God, not on the activity or
event in which one desires success.

This is so contrary to the world's way, but God's
people are called to a higher calling, a higher
standard, a different way. That higher, different
way is to be more concerned with what is pleasing to God rather than the world's concept of success.

9) God's plan for your success can be found in the Word of God.

It doesn't matter how the world defines success.
Such success is temporary anyway. However,
success by God's standards has eternal value!

It's so important that God revealed His plans
for your success in His Word.

Surely the Sovereign LORD does nothing without revealing his plan to his servants the prophets.

                                        Amos 3:7

Do not let this Book of the Law depart from your mouth; meditate on it day and night, so that you may be careful to do everything written in it. Then you will be prosperous and successful.

                                        Joshua 1:8

The purpose of God's Word is to reveal God. But in the process of revealing the nature of God, His Word gives us some practical, applicable truths that should be applied to our lives. Such truths will change us eternally. One of those significant truths is that God wants you to be successful and has designed your life for success.

Not only does He state that He intends for you to be successful, He gives you insight into how He desires you to succeed. As we've already seen, obedience to God is a prerequisite for success. The verse above (Joshua 1:8) makes that clear. But along with that prerequisite is a promise from God that total obedience to Him will produce success.

So what is the definition of success?

Success is the result of
accomplishing God's
plans and potential for
your life.

Success is the result of accomplishing God's plans and potential for your life.

Such a simple definition does not mean that the process is simple or that success is easy. In fact, just the opposite may be true. The process of success may be long and arduous. Success may be costly and difficult. That's not for you and me to decide. It's up to God.

On the other hand, the sheer joy of knowing that you are in the center of God's will, accomplishing what He wants you to accomplish while enjoying the presence and blessings of God, is a far greater pleasure than anything the world has to offer. The realization that we are being used by God for His purposes and plans is an indescribable reward. That moment of epiphany when we understand that we are part of an eternal plan of success without a doubt gives us the greatest sense of worth and value that we can possibly experience this side of heaven.

CHAPTER 2
GOD'S PATTERN OF SUCCESS

14 "Come together, all of you, and listen: Which of the idols has foretold these things? The LORD'S chosen ally will carry out his purposed against Babylon; his arm will be against the Babylonians.

15 I, even I, have spoken; yes, I have called him. I will bring him, and he will succeed in his mission.

16 "Come near me and listen to this: "From the first announcement I have not spoken in secret; at the time it happens, I am there."
And now the Sovereign LORD has sent me, endowed with his Spirit.

17 This is what the LORD says— your Redeemer, the Holy One of Israel: "I am the LORD your God, who teaches you what is best for you, who directs you in the way you should go.

Isaiah 48:14-17

Isaiah's fascinating passage gives us some insight into God's ways. God knows what is best for us, and He has plans to lead us in such a way. Sometimes His methods seem so strange and out-of-character, but the more we get to know God, the more we learn to expect the unexpected.

Right in the middle of this passage, verse 15, is a remarkable statement that reveals God's pattern of success. This is how He does it! This is the path He generally follows when leading us to success – to what is best for us.

Let's break this verse down to understand God's pattern of success.

"I, even I, have spoken...."

To be successful by God's standards, it is imperative to know what He has said concerning the matter. We are blessed to live at a point in history where we have God's Word to rely on. In order to succeed in a matter you must know what God has to say about it. You need to get into the Word and search out the mind of God.

Understand that the Word of God is given for one primary purpose: to know God. Everything else that one discovers in the Bible is contingent on that critical priority. In fact, all of the laws in the Bible, all of the principles, all of the promises, all of the stories, all of the history are secondary to the revelation of the person of God. As we get to know Him, all of the other matters in the Bible take on a fresh and powerful meaning.

Since God is the author of life, it makes sense that He knows how to get the most out of it. As His person is revealed in the Word, so are His views about life.

What does He have to say about the matter? What are the issues that He considers to be of utmost importance? What are His priorities? Has He already defined what success will be in the matter?

While you may think the Bible is difficult to understand, it is important to know that just as God inspired the writing of it, He also inspires the interpretation of it. The same Spirit that motivated and controlled the writing of this godly expression we call the Holy Bible also motivates and reveals His intent to those who seek His truths in it.

In fact, He gives us directions for understanding and getting the most out of His Word.

> *16 All Scripture is God-breathed and is useful for teaching, rebuking, correcting and training in righteousness,*
> *17 so that the man of God may be thoroughly equipped for every good work.*
> 2 Timothy 3:16-17

According to this passage, the way to study and get the most out of the Bible is to understand that all Scripture, in context, serves four purposes: to teach (doctrine), to rebuke (show us where we are wrong), to correct (show us how to right the wrong), and to train (show us the practical application).

As you study the Bible by those four guidelines, His Word will come alive for you. You'll begin to understand it in a way you never did before. And you will discover all those godly directives for success that are found throughout its pages.

"I have called him."

God's plan for success includes a calling. God calls you to success! This is not necessarily an emotional sense, although there may be emotion involved. More than likely there will not be bells and whistles and writing on the wall. You will probably not hear a thunderous voice from the heavens. No, a calling is greater than that. It is a sense of destiny...an awareness that God has appointed you to the matter...a confidence that cannot be defined...a certainty that God has assigned the task to you.

The Bible says a lot about one's calling.

... I urge you to live a life worthy of the calling you have received.

Ephesians 4:1

With this in mind, we constantly pray for you, that our God may count you worthy of his calling, and that by his power he may fulfill every good purpose of yours and every act prompted by your faith.

2 Thessalonians 1:11

To the church of God in Corinth, to those sanctified in Christ Jesus and called to be holy....

1 Corinthians 1:2

God, who has called you into fellowship with his Son Jesus Christ our Lord, is faithful.

1 Corinthians 1:9

You, my brothers, were called to be free.

Galatians 5:13

I pray also that the eyes of your heart may be enlightened in order that you may know the hope to which he has called you....

Ephesians 1:18

> *Do not repay evil with evil or insult with insult, but with blessing, because to this you were called so that you may inherit a blessing.*
>
> 1 Peter 3:9

> *And the God of all grace, who called you to his eternal glory in Christ, after you have suffered a little while, will himself restore you and make you strong, firm and steadfast.*
>
> 1 Peter 5:10

Note that these words are for all Christians, not just those who sense that God has set them aside for full-time ministry. We make a grave mistake in thinking that the only people who are "called" are those who enter into full-time church or missionary work.

We are *all* called. Notice what we are called to: a worthy life, a fulfilled purpose, holiness, fellowship with Christ, freedom, hope, blessing, and eternal glory! These are things that God has destined for you.

"I will bring him...."

This is one of the greatest assurances in the Bible. God is in control. He will bring the matter to pass. It is after all His success story that is being written. God is totally aware of the circumstances, the conflicts, and the consequences. He knows what has to happen to achieve the success He wants in your life. He has never failed and never will. Your job is to let Him "bring you" to success.

> *The one who calls you is faithful and He will do it.*
>
> 1 Thessalonians 5:24

Do what? Accomplish what He has called you to do.

What a great lesson this is. God doesn't just call you to your destiny; He intends to see you through it! This omniscient God already knows every obstacle you must face along the way, and He has already planned for it. God has already mapped out your success!

> *For it is God who works in you to will and to act according to his good purpose.*
>
> Philippians 2:13

Wow! What a great God! He not only reveals His will for you, He works in you to get it done according to His purpose.

God must get such great pleasure out of seeing His plan come together. That is exactly what He is looking for in your life. He's looking to see His plan come together in you. And when His will is accomplished in you He sees that as His "good purpose."

If you have His Word, if you have His calling, if you have His active control in the matter, what more do you need for success?

> *O LORD, save us; O LORD, grant us success.*
>
> Psalm 118:25

> *2 All a person's ways seem pure to them, but motives are weighed by the LORD.*
> *3 Commit to the LORD whatever you do, and he will establish your plans.*
> *4 The LORD works out everything to its proper end — even the wicked for a day of disaster.*
>
> Proverbs 16:2-4

So we know there are three things God does as He directs our success: He gives us His Word to direct us; He gives us a calling to clarify the direction we are to go; and He leads us ("brings" us) along the way.

Personally, this is the passage God used to clarify for me that He is my mentor.

If you have His Word,
if you have His calling,
if you have His active
control in the matter,
what more do you need
for success?

I realized a long time ago that my personal success would never be a textbook example. I would never be like the businessmen after whom I had sought to model myself.. God has simply taken me in another direction. My success is a stark contrast to the business models I have so admired. God had a different method in mind for me.

I'm really no different from anyone else in that regard. God's ways are so much higher and better than man's ways. If I had patterned myself after other men and women, I would have cheated myself of the pleasure of watching God work out His will and His ways.

> *As the heavens are higher than the earth, so are my ways higher than your ways and my thoughts than your thoughts.*
>   Isaiah 55:9

God's pattern of success is certainly different from most of the success strategies you can find in self-help books or on the Internet. I encourage you to seek His strategy for you. Don't be concerned with the way others have done it. I don't know of anyone who has been truly successful that followed someone else's methodology.

God's ways are unique. The way He has planned for you is unique. It has never been done before quite the way He has planned for you. Why? Because you are one of a kind; He has designed you and His plan for your life as a one-of-a-kind strategy!

So the secret of your success is to focus on His strategy, His ways, and His goals.

CHAPTER 3

THE POWER OF
GOAL SETTING

*Goal: accomplishing the intended result of
a specific focus, strategy, and effort*

Success is never an accident. It may come as a surprise, but it is never unintended.

Thomas Edison, possibly the greatest inventor of our time, owned 1,093 patents when he died. From the phonograph to power plants, his work has never been equaled. Some would say that his greatest invention was the incandescent light bulb.

However, what many people don't know is that for fifty years prior to Edison's accomplishment, other inventors had been experimenting with and developing forms of electric lighting. Edison found a way to harness that electricity and contain it in a filament that would work. He studied the work of the researchers and inventors before him. He did countless experiments and developed numerous designs before finding, in 1879, a type of filament that would burn within a vacuum globe for about thirteen hours.

In the process of developing the light bulb for which he became famous, he actually invented seven different related systems, including the parallel circuit, safety fuses, and light sockets with on/off switches. Each of these was critical to his success. Each system was a goal he had to accomplish before he could claim success in creating the incandescent light bulb.

Goals are the things you must accomplish in order to claim success.

For example, if you wanted to build a house, there would be a series of things you had to accomplish before you could say that you had built the house. Now, you might say that your goal is to build the house, but actually the house is the success of accomplishing several goals. Each of those goals has to be finished before you can claim success. Each goal has some unique criteria.

Goals identify and solve problems or needs.

An exterior wall solves many different problems or needs when building a house. It helps to hold up the roof. It keeps out wind and rain and cold.

It provides safety for the inhabitants. It defines space.

One of the key elements as you seek God's success for your life is to identify the needs that you must meet. Remember, the first principle of God's concept of success is to meet needs. Your goals should line up with that.

I was in a management meeting of a company I once worked for, and the CEO said, "Okay, regardless of the problems we might face, what are the things we want to see happen? Let's dream big!"

After much discussion, he had a list of about ten things on the whiteboard. Then the CEO said, "Now, those are our goals for the next twelve months."

Not one of the goals was based on meeting needs. They were all based on wants.

Not one of the goals was accomplished.

Define your needs and your needs will define your goals.

Goals allow for failure.

Through the years we have learned better ways to build walls, but that process has come at the expense of many failures. However, it would be unfair to say those failures were unaccomplished goals. They were actually part of the process of accomplishing each goal. Failure is an integral part of accomplishing goals.

Define your needs and
your needs will define
your goals.

When understood, failure is the discovery of something that is counterproductive to the intended success. Thomas Edison had far more failures than accomplished goals. In fact, more than fifty years of failure by Edison and other researchers preceded the discovery of that one filament that worked. Think about it: one accomplished goal for thousands of failures!

It has been said that Edison often laughed at a failed experiment, saying, "Well, there's another way that it won't work!"

A failure is not the loss of success. If anything, it is a step toward success because it is a discovery of how not to do it. Think about it: failure is another step in discovering success. That makes it part of what a goal is all about.

Understand that there are positive failures and negative failures. Generally, they are a matter of perspective.

Positive failures help to point us in the right direction. They show us the way *not* to go. They reveal another parameter to keep us from failing in that way again. For example, once on a road trip with my family I decided to take what appeared on the map as a shortcut. It wasn't. Although the drive was quite beautiful, I ended up spending an extra three hours weaving through the mountains much to my wife's

chagrin and my children's consternation. You
can be sure I never took that route again. It
was a positive failure.

Negative failures create loss and limitations.
For example, I had a friend who decided to
build an addition on his house. Unfortunately,
he didn't prepare the ground appropriately.
About the time he was finishing the project, he
noticed that the room had started to sink into
the ground. Now, while he learned from his
mistake, he still suffered a rather significant
loss of time, energy, and money. That's a negative failure.

Goals are in effect the process of perfection. But
perfection is never achieved without overcoming
the obstacles and failures that defy such perfection.

A goal allows for failure.

Goals must be accomplished in order.

You wouldn't build your roof first and then try to
build your walls. That would be counterproductive. And you certainly wouldn't want to try to
build your foundation after you had put up the
walls.

There must be an order to goals. Certain goals cannot be accomplished until other goals have been reached.

Goals must have order.

Goals maintain their value.

Once you have finished building a wall for your house, that wall must continue to stand to be effective and useful. You may decide to modify the wall, but the original intent still continues to maintain its purpose.

A completed goal has value.

Consider the realistic value of each of your goals.

Goals are motivated by purpose.

When building a house, each element has a purpose. Steps have a purpose—you don't just build a set of steps to nowhere. Doors have a unique purpose; windows have a unique purpose. Windows don't make good doors. Doors don't make good windows—especially on the second floor of the house!

Goals have purpose.

So goals are the process of achieving success.
They are crucial. There really is no success without accomplishing goals.

How important are goals?

God has goals.

It's true. God has goals. He always has.

He is an orderly God who abides by His goals.
Your goals are really nothing more than deter-
mining how you fit in with God's plan and accomplishing your role.

God actually has a plan and a system.

> *But the plans of the LORD stand firm for-
> ever, the purposes of his heart through all
> generations.*
>
> Psalm 33:11

> *"For I know the plans I have for you," de-
> clares the LORD, "plans to prosper you and
> not to harm you, plans to give you hope and
> a future."*
>
> Jeremiah 29:11

One of the interesting principles in the Bible is
that God has goals for you. You are part of God's
eternal plan!

You hem me in—behind and before; you have laid your hand upon me.

Psalm 139:5

...Your hand will guide me, your right hand will hold me fast.

Psalm 139:10

11 In him we were also chosen, having been predestined according to the plan of him who works out everything in conformity with the purpose of his will,
12 in order that we, who were the first to put our hope in Christ, might be for the praise of his glory.

Ephesians 1:11-12

This was a life-changing revelation for me.

You see, I was a mistake. I never should have been born. At least that's what I thought.

I was born to an unmarried teenage mother. I don't know the circumstances of her pregnancy; I only know she must have been scared and lonely. But she did the smartest thing she could have done: she gave me up for adoption.

A young couple in seminary studying to be missionaries had been praying and preparing to adopt a baby. God put us together. He took what could have been a disastrous situation and turned it into good. It was God's protection for me along with His answer to the prayers of a young child-less couple—and, in a way, a gift to that young mother.

A few years later something wonderful happened. While on the mission field, my parents got pregnant. Several times! I think that's one of the reasons they tell you not to drink the water when you're in a foreign country!

I was never made to feel less loved. In fact, my parents went out of their way to tell me how special I was to them and how much they loved me. But in my nine-year-old mind I began to question how my parents could possibly love me as much as they loved their own flesh and blood.

As I played that over and over in my head I began to see myself as a mistake that my parents had rescued. And I started to think of myself as "second-class." I remember thinking *I shouldn't even exist. I'm an accident.*

That went on for years. I grew very bitter and at times despondent. The natural step was to believe that I had no purpose in life, no reason for living.

During my third year of college I met a young man who confronted me with one very simple question: "Why do you exist?"

I never told him what was going on in my head, but he went on to follow up his first question with "Have you ever wondered why you are one-of-a-kind? There's no one else in the world like you, there never has been, and there never will be. Why do you suppose that is?"

I really didn't want to have that conversation, but I couldn't get away from it. He then gave me a verse from the Bible:

> *You are worthy, our Lord and God, to receive glory and honor and power, for you created all things, and by your will they were created and have their being.*
> Revelation 4:11

It suddenly dawned on me what that verse meant: I was created by the will of God. I wasn't illegitimate! My birth-parents may have been illegitimate, but I wasn't! God planned me.

I started looking in the Bible for more about this amazing truth. Somehow I ended up in the Psalms, and I read:

> *13 For you created my inmost being; you knit me together in my mother's womb.*
> *14 I praise you because I am fearfully and wonderfully made; your works are wonderful, I know that full well.*
> *15 My frame was not hidden from you when I was made in the secret place, when I was woven together in the depths of the earth.*

> *16 Your eyes saw my unformed body; all the days ordained for me were written in your book before one of them came to be.*
>
> Psalm 139:13-16

Wow! God knew me *before* my body was even formed, and He "ordained" my days before I was born. I wasn't a mistake! I wasn't an accident as far as God is concerned. He had a plan and purpose for my life!

Yes, God has a plan. He has a purpose. He has goals. And the wonderful truth is that you are part of His goals. You are included in His plan.

Jesus had goals.

> *He replied, "Go tell that fox, 'I will drive out demons and heal people today and tomorrow, and on the third day I will reach my goal.'"*
>
> Luke 13:32

Jesus understood that He had things to do "today" and things to do "tomorrow."

Each day was a step toward His goal. Each day became its own goal. Each circumstance became part of His goal.

You are part of Jesus' goal. In John 10:10 Jesus said of Himself, "...I have come that they may have life, and have it to the full." He was talking

about His goal. He was talking about His goal
for you. His goal was that you have a fulfilled
life. His goal was that you get the most out of
life—every day!

What an amazing statement. Jesus' goal for
your life is that you live it to the fullest, and that's
why He came to earth and did what He did! His
goal is for you to become everything that God the
Father designed for you. He sees you as a "child
of destiny," and His mission is to make sure you
fulfill your destiny.

Paul had goals.

The apostle Paul took planning and goal setting
very seriously. His background was one of great
discipline and commitment. He understood the
power of goal setting.

> *When I planned this, did I do it lightly?*
> 2 Corinthians 1:17

Paul's goal was to please God.

> *And without faith it is impossible to*
> *please God, because anyone who comes to*
> *him must believe that he exists and that*
> *he rewards those who earnestly seek him.*
> Hebrews 11:6

Paul sought to please Him in life. He discovered that's really the only way that life means anything. That's how God designed us. Your life can only be fulfilled as you please God. Your life will have meaning only as you please God.

> *Finally, brothers, we instructed you how to live in order to please God, as in fact you are living. Now we ask you and urge you in the Lord Jesus to do this more and more.*
>
> 1 Thessalonians 4:1

Paul sought to please Him in death.

> *So we make it our goal to please him, whether we are at home in the body or away from it.*
>
> 2 Corinthians 5:9

A few years ago, my home church went through a rather paradoxical week. Within days of each other, we held the funeral of a famous baseball player who apparently died from a drug overdose, and the funeral of an elderly man who died of natural causes. The first enjoyed great riches and a successful life by the world's standards. The latter spent sixty years volunteering at the City Union Mission and devoted his life to raising a family by godly standards. It's pretty obvious which one pleased God in his death.

One apparently lived his life for himself and his own ambition. The other had one passion: to please God. God honored that older man's commitment. His children, and grandchildren, and great-grandchildren continue to seek the Lord and be faithful to him, and God has blessed them.

What are your goals?

What does God want to accomplish in and through you? What do you want to accomplish in your life?

Take a moment to think about and write down your answers to those questions.

Realistically, how can you take the next step toward success if you don't know the answers to these questions?

Let me recommend that you stop reading at this point and take the time to discover these answers. Carve out some time by yourself where you can think this through. Write down your answers on a separate sheet of paper. You may find that what you first write down is not what you really believe is right for your life. And it's possible that you just can't think of any long-term goals right now. That's okay.

We tend to think of goals as lofty, noble, life-impacting, world-changing efforts. In my seminars I use terms like "Power Goals" and

"Success Strategies." However, as I'm writing this chapter, my wife Marcia just paused on her way down to the laundry room and said, "My Power Goal and Success Strategy for today is to get the laundry done."

I feel rather humbled.

Anyway, at some point as you begin thinking about what God has in store for you, your long-term goals will start to come into focus. When that happens, follow your heart.

Once you have an idea of what your goals are, think about this: what does God have to do first in your life? In other words, what do you have to do to accomplish your intent? What does God have to do to accomplish His intent?

Perhaps another way of asking it is what has to happen for your goals to line up with God's? What has to happen for your goals to be the same as God's goals for you?

Your primary goal should be to please God!

> *I press on toward the goal to win the prize for which God has called me heavenward in Christ Jesus.*
>
> Philippians 3:14

The apostle Paul understood this very key principle. Your primary goal should be all about pleasing God.

CHAPTER 4

THE GOAL OF PLEASING GOD

What does it mean to please God?

Just as Paul's goal was to please God, so should each of us seek that same lofty goal.

This is one of the greatest concepts in the Bible—that God's children bring Him pleasure. It makes sense. We see it in a limited way between the earthly child and parent. When a child does something well or obedient or delightful the parents take great pleasure in that.

In a far greater way, God takes pleasure in His children. He takes great delight in His children who do things right or well or in obedience. And just as such behavior puts a smile on a parent's face, so too God must smile at His children.

That may well be the concept behind what the Bible refers to as "seeking the face of God." In

other words, look to see if God is pleased; see if
He has a smile on His face.

> *Look to the LORD and his strength; seek
> his face always.*
>
> 1 Chronicles 16:11

> *...if my people, who are called by my
> name, will humble themselves and pray
> and seek my face and turn from their
> wicked ways, then will I hear from heav-
> en and will forgive their sin and will heal
> their land.*
>
> 2 Chronicles 7:14

> *My heart says of you, "Seek his face!" Your
> face, LORD, I will seek.*
>
> Psalm 27:8

> *Look to the LORD and his strength; seek
> his face always.*
>
> Psalm 105:4

Well, what puts a smile on God's face?

> *3 Who may ascend the hill of the LORD?
> Who may stand in his holy place?
> 4 He who has clean hands and a pure
> heart, who does not lift up his soul to an idol
> or swear by what is false.*

*5 He will receive blessing from the LORD
and vindication from God his Savior.
6 Such is the generation of those who seek
him, <u>who seek your face</u>, O God of Jacob.*
                        Psalm 24:3-6 (emphasis added)

Those who seek the face of God—who seek to put a smile on His face—are those who have "clean hands and a pure heart," who keep themselves from idolatry (anything that is a substitute for God), and are honest and have integrity. Such a person will "receive blessing from the Lord" and "ascend the hill of the LORD" and "stand in His holy place." In other words, such a person will receive all that a God who is pleased has to offer!

God is committed to revealing Himself to those who seek Him.

*19 ...what may be known about God is plain to them, because God has made it plain to them.
20 For since the creation of the world God's invisible qualities—his eternal power and divine nature—have been clearly seen, being understood from what has been made, so that people are without excuse.*
                        Romans 1:19-20

The desire to please God will result in the blessing of God's success.

The desire to please God will result in the blessing of God's success.

Live to please God.

So living to please God is critical to success. However, pleasing God doesn't come naturally. Our
natural way of doing things is to please self.

Pleasing God is learned.

> *Finally, brothers, we instructed you how to*
> *live in order to please God....*
>
> 1 Thessalonians 4:1

Learning to please God comes from being instructed in His Word, from getting to know God,
and from spending time with Him.

That makes sense. The more time you spend
with someone, the more you learn about that person, the more you get to know them, the more you
discover what they like and dislike.

I've heard many older couples say that one of
the keys to their long and successful relationship is that they never stopped learning more
about each other. The same is true with God.
You can never know all there is to know about
Him; He is always willing to reveal more.

The more you get to know Him, the greater will
be your desire to please Him. Conversely, the
more you please God, the more opportunities you
will have to please Him.

On the other hand, God identifies in His Word a
few things that displease Him. In order to live a

life that seeks to please Him, we must know what displeases Him.

Dishonesty displeases God.

> *The LORD detests differing weights, and dishonest scales do not please him.*
>
> Proverbs 20:23

Some would argue that honesty and dishonesty are relative, that they are ambiguous, and that what may be honest for one person is dishonest for another. Such arguments are based on man's philosophies.

The bottom line is what does God think about it?

When He is the standard for our lives, anything less than His character and way of doing things is unacceptable. God doesn't think in terms of indiscretions and incomplete truths. For God, anything less than total honesty is dishonesty.

Now, note that we are not talking about tact and protocol here. We are talking about character. God is displeased with a dishonest character. In effect, He is displeased with any character that allows for lying, stealing, cheating, or dishonesty.

A sinful nature cannot please God.

> *Those controlled by the sinful nature can-*
> *not please God.*
> Romans 8:8

Just what is a sinful nature? In order to understand that we have to understand what sin
is.

Most people would define sin as doing the
wrong thing. It is, however, far more dangerous
than that. Sin is deadly. It required the sacrificial death of animals in the Old Testament. It
caused the sacrificial death of Jesus in the New
Testament.

Sin has often been defined as "missing the mark"
based on Romans 3:23 – "for all have sinned and
fall short of the glory of God." However, that definition misses the mark.

Sin is not just having a bad aim. Sin is the condition of being out of God's will. Sin is missing the
whole point of why you were created and what
God's purpose for your life is all about. Sin is missing out on everything that God has planned for
you!

I like the illustration of sin being the ocean
around an island. Picture an island representing

God's will. The ocean around the island is sin. Sin is the state of being off the island of God's will.

While out in the ocean of sin, you find the results of being off the island reveal themselves in such things as lying, stealing, cheating, etc. The lying and stealing and cheating are the revelation of the condition of sin. Being off the island of God's will is the sin. So sin is the condition of being out of God's will, and that condition may reveal itself in a number of different actions. The important thing to understand is that sin is a condition.

There are a lot of good people who never lie, steal, cheat, etc. But they are off the island of God's will. Even though they never do anything morally wrong, they are still in sin because they are "off the island."

Sin is being out of God's will. Repentance is getting back into God's will.

Back to the question: what is a sinful nature?

The sinful nature seeks fulfillment and pleasure away from God's will. Doing so is a displeasure to God.

God is not pleased with fools.

This is a rather peculiar statement, but it's true. God makes it very clear in His Word:

...He has no pleasure in fools....
                                    Ecclesiastes 5:4

What does that mean? The Bible defines a fool in some rather interesting ways.

That same verse in Ecclesiastes indicates that a fool is one who makes promises to God but doesn't keep them.

The Bible says that an atheist is a fool:

> *The fool says in his heart, "There is no God." They are corrupt, their deeds are vile; there is no one who does good.*
>   Psalm 14:1

Proverbs 10:18 says that *"...whoever spreads slander is a fool."* And verse 23 says, *"A fool finds pleasure in evil conduct...."*

Proverbs 14:16 says that *"a fool is hotheaded and reckless."*

A fool is undisciplined according to Proverbs 15:5 – *"A fool spurns his father's discipline...."*

A fool is opinionated without knowing all the facts:

> *A fool finds no pleasure in understanding but delights in airing his own opinions.*
>   Proverbs 18:2

A fool speaks of perverse things:

> *Better a poor man whose walk is blameless than a fool whose lips are perverse.*
>
> Proverbs 19:1

A fool is hotheaded and loves to quarrel according to Proverbs 20:3 – "...*every fool is quick to quarrel.*"

Proverbs 26:11 says a fool makes the same mistakes over and over: "...*a fool repeats his folly.*"

A fool can't control his anger.

> *A fool gives full vent to his anger, but a wise man keeps himself under control.*
>
> Proverbs 29:11

A fool has no common sense.

> *Even as he walks along the road, the fool lacks sense and shows everyone how stupid he is.*
>
> Ecclesiastes 10:3

No wonder God is displeased with fools.

A lifestyle of meaningless worship displeases God.

> *11 "The multitude of your sacrifices— what are they to me?" says the LORD. "I have more than enough of burnt offerings, of rams and the fat of fattened animals; I have no pleasure in the blood of bulls and lambs and goats.*
>
> *16 Wash and make yourselves clean. Take your evil deeds out of my sight; stop doing wrong.*
>
> *17 Learn to do right; seek justice. Defend the oppressed. Take up the cause of the fatherless; plead the case of the widow.*
>
> Isaiah 1:11,16-17

This is critical. The Bible makes a number of references to meaningless worship and how displeased God is with it. In every case, the worshippers suffered dire consequences. The amazing thing is that in each example the worshippers thought they were doing it right.

Worship is extremely important. It's so important that if it's done wrong, God is displeased. In this passage from Isaiah, God makes it clear that style and effort are inconsequential. Sincere worship that is wrong is sincerely wrong. God doesn't make allowances for sincerity. He doesn't think "Aw, poor guys. They just don't know any better. At least they're sincere."

Wrong is wrong.

This passage makes it clear that worship is a lifestyle. It's not just something you do on Sunday morning in church. Worship is the result of God having the right position in your life and you having the right position in God's life. The result is revealed in a number of ways.

The first way mentioned in this passage from Isaiah is confession of sin: *"...wash and make yourselves clean...."*

So the first act of worship is to **confess our sin** and get back into God's will. First John 1:9 says that *"If we confess our sins, he is faithful and just and will forgive us our sins and purify us from all unrighteousness."*

This promise from God assures us that He will receive our confession and make us right with Him. The forgiveness is immediate. The cleansing, or "purification," may take awhile. But God is able and willing to do just what He says He will.

The second act of worship is to **commit ourselves to purity**: *"...Take your evil deeds out of my sight!"*

In other words, quit doing those things that are offensive to God. Since nothing is out of God's sight, the only way to keep an evil act out of His sight is to not do it.

The third element of worship is **discovery**.

...Stop doing wrong, learn to do right!
Isaiah 1:16-17

Actually, the Hebrew word for "right" here is the word for justice. The implication is that we are to operate by the standard of God's truth. Doing right doesn't come naturally. It has to be learned. It has to be taught. That, of course, comes through the Word of God.

The fourth element of worship mentioned in Isaiah 1:16-17 is to **meet needs** – *"Seek justice, encourage the oppressed. Defend the cause of the fatherless, plead the case of the widow."*

As we saw earlier in this book, it is the nature of God to meet needs. True worship produces the nature of the worshipped in the worshipper. As we worship God, whose nature is to meet needs, our desire will also be to meet needs.

So what pleases God?

The Word declares a number of specific things that please God. If our desire is to please Him, we do well to heed these.

God is pleased with integrity.

King David noted it this way:

> *I know, my God, that you test the heart and are pleased with integrity....*
> 1 Chronicles 29:17

Integrity is part of one's character. It means that one does "the right thing." Not because it's easier or more accommodating. Not because one fears the consequences of doing the wrong thing. But simply because it's the right thing to do.

God is pleased with your personal fulfillment.

> ...*The LORD be exalted, who delights in the well-being of his servant.*
> Psalm 35:27

But note that God is pleased with the personal fulfillment of "His servant." The implication must be absorbed. Personal fulfillment when we are serving God is of great delight to Him. God seeks the personal fulfillment of those that serve Him!

God is pleased with reverence.

> *The LORD delights in those who fear him, who put their hope in his unfailing love.*
> Psalm 147:11

The word "fear" in this verse actually means "to revere." It doesn't mean being afraid but rather being overcome with awe. While that may mean that one should be fearful if he is out of the will of God, the intent is that one should be mesmerized with the holiness and greatness of God.

God is pleased with His people.

> *For the LORD takes delight in his people; he crowns the humble with salvation.*
>
> Psalm 149:4

God actually enjoys His people – those who have a personal relationship with Him. We may also assume the converse: God does not take pleasure in those who are not His own.

God is pleased for His people to exercise His authority.

God takes pleasure in turning His authority over to us:

> *...it is your Father's good pleasure to give you the kingdom....*
>
> Luke 12:32

Of course with that authority comes the responsibility to manage your authority appropriately.

God is pleased by your requests, prayers, intercession, and thanksgiving.

1 I urge, then, first of all, that petitions, prayers, intercession and thanksgiving be made for all people—
2 for kings and all those in authority, that we may live peaceful and quiet lives in all godliness and holiness.
3 This is good, and pleases God our Savior.
1 Timothy 2:1-3

What an amazing truth! God loves it when you share your requests, prayers, intercessions, and thanksgiving with Him.

Now I know this verse is referring to prayers for authority figures, but the principle is still the same: God wants to answer your prayers! He is pleased when you bring your concerns to Him.

God is pleased by your faith.

God gets excited about your faith!

Without faith it is impossible to please God.
Hebrews 11:6

Your faith is critical to your success because it is important to God. God loves for you to trust

Him! When you do that it gives Him permission to do what He wants to do.

So if we know what pleases God, how can we put those things into practice?

How Can We Please God?

The apostle Paul identified several things that please God.

> *10 so that you may live a life worthy of the Lord and please him in every way: bearing fruit in every good work, growing in the knowledge of God,*
>
> *11 being strengthened with all power according to his glorious might so that you may have great endurance and patience,*
>
> *12 and giving joyful thanks to the Father, who has qualified you to share in the inheritance of his holy people in the kingdom of light.*
>
> Colossians 1:10-12

Now, mark this point in the book because we're going to take a look at each one of these things that pleases God. It will take several pages and you might want to refer back to these three verses every once in awhile.

Paul understood that we need a handle on this concept of pleasing God. So here he points out some ways that we are pleasing to Him.

"Bearing fruit"

This point alone can change your life. Why? Because it goes against the grain of everything we've been taught about how to succeed.

Generally, we're told that to succeed one must work hard, work smart, and enjoy a little luck. But here Jesus says that success is like a grapevine.

Now picture this: as the grapevine grows it produces fruit. Jesus likens success to the cluster of grapes. But how does that cluster of grapes happen?

Does it have to work hard?

Does it have to work smart?

Does it have to be lucky?

Of course the answer to each of these questions is no. And that is basic to understanding how God will bring about success in your life. This is how Jesus explained it:

> 1"I am the true vine, and my Father is the gardener.
> 2 He cuts off every branch in me that bears no fruit, while every branch that does bear fruit he prunes so that it will be even more fruitful.

*3 You are already clean because of the word
I have spoken to you.
4 Remain in me, as I also remain in you.
No branch can bear fruit by itself; it must
remain in the vine. Neither can you bear
fruit unless you remain in me.
5 "I am the vine; you are the branches. If
you remain in me and I in you, you will
bear much fruit; apart from me you can do
nothing.
6 If you do not remain in me, you are like
a branch that is thrown away and withers;
such branches are picked up, thrown into
the fire and burned.
7 If you remain in me and my words remain in you, ask whatever you wish, and it
will be done for you.
8 This is to my Father's glory, that you bear
much fruit, showing yourselves to be my
disciples.
9 "As the Father has loved me, so have I
loved you. Now remain in my love.
10 If you keep my commands, you will remain in my love, just as I have kept my
Father's commands and remain in his
love."*

John 15:1-10

So how does the branch produce fruit? It doesn't.
It simply *bears* the fruit.

Do you see the magnificent truth here? Success is not the result of working hard and slaving away until you finally see some results. That may be the world's way, but it is certainly not God's way.

Now, take a moment and ponder this. For years you have been told that to be successful you have to work harder than everybody else, work smarter than everybody else, and have a little luck on your side. And all along you've known that philosophy just didn't seem to line up with what God wanted from your life. Why?

The simple truth is that God has never asked you to be successful. He's asked you to be obedient. That is the foundation of real success. The result of your obedience is that it gives God the freedom to do what He wants—to accomplish what He desires. The result is the "fruit" mentioned in this verse.

That fruit, and not what you produce, pleases God.

Well, what is that fruit specifically?

22 But the fruit of the Spirit is love, joy, peace, forbearance, kindness, goodness, faithfulness,
23 gentleness and self-control. Against such things there is no law.

Galatians 5:22-23

The simple truth is that God has never asked you to be successful. He's asked you to be obedient. That is the foundation of real success.

This is such an awesome principle. This is what God is trying to develop in your life. It's actually a picture of the character of God. People who fight this are of all people most unsuccessful.

What do these elements mean? Why are they so important? The following is a list of these words, followed by the Greek word and its applied meaning:

Love – *agape* – allowing God to do something in someone else's life through you

Joy – *chara* – calm and enlightened contentment

Peace – *eirene* – quiet rest / "at one" / implies prosperity

Longsuffering – *makrothumia* – patient fortitude

Gentleness – *chrestotes* – moral kindness

Goodness – *agathosune* – virtuous benevolence

Faith – *pistis* – trusting obedience to the known will of God

Meekness – *praiotes* – humble gentleness

Temperance – *egkrateia* – in strength / self-control / empowered

"Against such there is no law"—in other words, there is no law, no *thing*, you can do to create these elements in your life. You can't MAKE yourself have these character traits. They are

the "fruit" of the Spirit, and they develop in your life as the Spirit of God lives in and through you.

To fully understand what this means, we have to go back earlier in Galatians 5 to see a contrast that Paul draws.

> *19 The acts of the flesh are obvious: sexual immorality, impurity and debauchery;*
> *20 idolatry and witchcraft; hatred, discord, jealousy, fits of rage, selfish ambition, dissensions, factions*
> *21 and envy; drunkenness, orgies, and the like. I warn you, as I did before, that those who live like this will not inherit the kingdom of God.*
>
> Galatians 5:19-21

Now that we've taken a look at the contrast in Galatians 5 between man's nature (vv. 19-21) and the nature of God (vv. 22-23) it is important to understand that either way is a choice to live accordingly.

If you choose to live under the control of your sinful nature you can expect your life to be filled with any combination of "sexual immorality (whether it be simple impurities or total debauchery), idolatry and witchcraft (including drug abuse – the Greek word for witchcraft is *pharmakeia*); hatred, discord (strife and contention), jealousy, fits of rage (uncontrolled fierceness), selfish ambition, dissensions (disunity), factions (disunity caused by heresy) and envy (jealousy resulting in ill-will); drunkenness, orgies, and the like."

If you choose to live under the control of the vine, bearing the fruit of the Spirit, you can expect your life to be filled with *agape* love (allowing God to do something in someone else's life through you), joy (calm delight in God), peace (at one – quiet rest), longsuffering (patience), gentleness (moral kindness), goodness (godly virtue), faith (trusting obedience to the known will of God), meekness (humble strength), and self-control. These are not things that you control. These are things that God produces in your life. You can't make them happen. You can't follow a bunch of rules and make them appear. There is no biblical "formula" to make these things real in your life.

Note one other thing about the fruit of the Spirit. The branch may find some satisfaction in bearing fruit, but the real benefit of the fruit is enjoyed by those who partake of it—that person with whom you work who really needs some gentleness, that family member who needs some *agape* love, that friend who notices your joy, that person you don't even know who is observing your faith, your "trusting obedience to the known will of God." The fruit is for their benefit!

This is a unique principle and truth. The orange tree doesn't eat its own oranges. The grapevine doesn't partake of its own grapes. The benefit of the fruit is enjoyed by others.

Do you realize what that means? Your success is for the benefit of others!

This is probably one of the most misunderstood principles of success. While you may claim success, true godly success is for the benefit of others!

Now certainly you will enjoy that success. You will appreciate some of the results of what God has done in your life. But the real benefit of your success will be enjoyed and appreciated by others.

"Growing in knowledge of God"

Continuing in our study of Colossians 1:10-12, and how we can please God, we see that growing in the knowledge of God is pleasing to Him.

This is such a glorious, powerful truth: you can know God! Not just know about Him, but actually *know* Him! Not only that, but He *wants* you to know Him!

It's not a pipedream. It's not a theory. It's a fact.

The problem most Christians have with getting to know God is that their knowledge is based on what someone else has told them. They're like the kids running around the pool wanting to jump in because everyone in the pool is having so much fun, but they're not sure if they can, or if they're ready, or even if they should. And once in the pool, then what? This is exactly how too many Christians live their lives.

God's Word is very clear on this matter. He wants us to know Him!

> *2 Grace and peace be yours in abundance through the knowledge of God and of Jesus our Lord.*
> *3 His divine power has given us everything we need for a godly life through our knowledge of him who called us by his own glory and goodness.*
>
> 2 Peter 1:2-3

So how do you get to know God?

Proverbs has great instruction on this matter:

> *1 My son, if you accept my words and store up my commands within you,*
> *2 turning your ear to wisdom and applying your heart to understanding —*
> *3 indeed, if you call out for insight and cry aloud for understanding,*

*4 and if you look for it as for silver and
search for it as for hidden treasure,
5 then you will understand the fear of the
LORD and find the knowledge of God.*
Proverbs 2:1-5

First, get into the Word of God. Study God's Word
and memorize the passages that are important to
you. For example, if you are struggling with re-
jection, find Scripture that reveals how much God
loves you and accepts you, and begin memorizing
some of those verses that jump out at you.

Secondly, apply the Word of God to your life.
That is what wisdom is: the applied knowledge
and understanding of God. What good does knowing the Word of God do if you're not applying it?
So when you find a passage of Scripture that
gives you direction, apply it appropriately. Do it!

For example, when Ephesians 4:26 says *"In
your anger do not sin: Do not let the sun go down
while you are still angry, and do not give the devil
a foothold"* its meaning is pretty obvious. Don't
let your anger control you and cause you to sin.
Get rid of the anger quickly. Make it a point not
to carry the anger beyond the end of the day, because if you do you give the devil a foothold in
your life to gain control over you.

So get into the Word of God and start applying it in your life. As you do you will discover the

nature and character of God. He will become very real to you. You will begin to know Him.

Thirdly, make knowing God a priority in your life. Pray for His insight and understanding. Seek those things as you would seek valuable treasure, because they are in fact treasure. Then as you seek such insight, God will reveal Himself and you will begin to really know God.

There is a wonderful promise from God concerning when He will reveal Himself:

> *And without faith it is impossible to please God, because anyone who comes to Him must believe that He exists and that He rewards those who earnestly seek Him.*
>
> Hebrews 11:6

Did you catch that last phrase? "…He rewards those who earnestly seek Him."

This is a very simple cause-and-effect statement. As you come to God in faith, He will reward you—He rewards those who seek Him.

Now think about it. What is the reward of those who seek diamonds? Diamonds, right? What is the reward of those who seek gold? I'm thinking probably gold. So what is the reward of those who seek God?

Of course! God Himself! As you seek to know Him, He will reveal Himself.

That God will reveal Himself is a promise repeated several times in the Bible.

> *The LORD looks down from heaven on the sons of men to see if there are any who understand, any who seek God.*
>
> Psalm 14:2

> *But if from there you seek the LORD your God, you will find him if you look for him with all your heart and with all your soul.*
>
> Deuteronomy 4:29

Both 1 Chronicles 28:9 and 2 Chronicles 15:2 say *"If you seek him, he will be found by you...."*

> *...those who seek the LORD lack no good thing.*
>
> Psalm 34:10

Seeking God leads to knowing God. Knowing God means that you not only know Him personally, but you know His ways, His will, His character. The prophet Jeremiah gave us a great example when he spoke of Josiah:

> *15 "Does it make you a king to have more and more cedar? Did not your father have*

*food and drink? He did what was right and
just, so all went well with him.
16 He defended the cause of the poor and
needy, and so all went well. Is that not what
it means to know me?" declares the LORD.*

Jeremiah 22:15-16

Paul wrote to the church in Ephesus about
knowing God:

*17 So I tell you this, and insist on it in the
Lord, that you must no longer live as the
Gentiles do, in the futility of their thinking.
18 They are darkened in their understanding and separated from the life of God because of the ignorance that is in them due
to the hardening of their hearts.
19 Having lost all sensitivity, they have
given themselves over to sensuality so as to
indulge in every kind of impurity, with a
continual lust for more.
20 You, however, did not come to <u>know</u>
Christ that way.
21 Surely you heard of him and were taught
in him in accordance with the truth that is
in Jesus.
22 You were taught, with regard to your
former way of life, to put off your old self,
which is being corrupted by its deceitful
desires;*

> *23 to be made new in the attitude of your minds;*
> *24 and to put on the new self, created to be like God in true righteousness and holiness.*
>   Ephesians 4:17-24 (emphasis added)

God is pleased for His children to know and love Him. As you get to know and love Him, you will discover greater blessings and truth that He has reserved for you!

> *...No eye has seen, no ear has heard, no mind has conceived what God has prepared for those who love him.*
>   1 Corinthians 2:9

Back to our study of the things that please God mentioned in Colossians 1:10-12.

"Being strengthened with all power"

Another way that we please God is by allowing Him to strengthen us with His own power.

In other words, quit trying to live life on your own. You don't have enough strength to do it on your own. You don't! Oh, you might have enough to get by for awhile, but sooner or later you're going to run out of the power you need to get through the tough times as well as the good times.

God is pleased to empower you with *His* power – not a secondary source of strength to draw on, but His own personal power!

This power was made available to you when you turned your life over to Christ:

> *I am not ashamed of the gospel, because it is the power of God for the salvation of everyone who believes: first for the Jew, then for the Gentile.*
>
> Romans 1:16

> *Having been buried with him in baptism and raised with him through your faith in the power of God, who raised him from the dead.*
>
> Colossians 2:12

That pastor/friend I referred to in the introduction of this book, Dr. Lew Miller, loved to teach this principle by taking a ball and glove with him to the pulpit. At some point during his message he would take out the ball and glove and lay the glove on the floor, saying, "This is how most Christians try to live their life. We want to do what God tells us to do, but we just can't."

Then he would say, "Now, glove, catch the ball." And he would toss the ball at the glove lying on the floor. Of course the ball would bounce off the glove and roll along the floor to everyone's amusement.

He would explain that many of us are like the glove. We want to do what we are designed to do, just as the glove is designed to catch the ball. But we can't. Something is missing.

Then he would pick up the glove and quote from Philippians:

> *I can do everything through him who gives me strength.*
>
> Philippians 4:13

Next he would hold up his hand and say, "Let my hand represent the strength of God. What we need is the strength of God *in* us to do what we are designed to do." He would then put his hand in the glove, toss the ball to himself, and catch it.

What a great example of what it means to be strengthened with the power of God!

Quit trying to live your life on your own power. You're wasting time and energy, and you'll never be successful doing it that way.

God empowers you with His own power so that you will be successful and He will be honored – not you; He will be recognized – not you; He will be praised – not you.

God empowers you
with His own power so
that you will be
successful and He
will be honored – not
you; He will be
recognized – not you;
He will be praised – not
you.

If anyone speaks, he should do it as one speaking the very words of God. If anyone serves, he should do it with the strength God provides, so that in all things God may be praised through Jesus Christ. To him be the glory and the power for ever and ever. Amen.

1 Peter 4:11

"Have great endurance and patience"

What? You mean I have to put up with stuff I don't like for a long time, and that pleases God?

Well, sort of.

It's interesting that these two words are used here since they are so similar. However, each is a little different. The word for endurance means fortitude over a period of time. The word for patience actually means a hopeful patience. Each characteristic needs the other.

The verses we're pivoting on as we study the things that please God (Colossians 1:10-12) say that great endurance and patience come from the strength we receive from the power of God. In other words, just as we cannot accomplish what we are designed by God to do unless we have His strength in us, so too we cannot have great endurance and patience unless we have His strength.

That endurance and patience which pleases God—and which you need in your life—comes from God! You don't have to muster it up and grit your teeth and hold on for dear life. That's not the endurance and patience that God is looking for.

The endurance and patience that pleases God acknowledges that He is in control in spite of the circumstances of your life. It doesn't mean you should be giddy about the bad things that happen. Of course not. Rather, it means that you know God is in control of your life; He is still on the throne and He still has a purpose and plan to accomplish through you.

Paul explained it this way in his letter to the church in Rome:

> *1 Therefore, since we have been justified through faith, we have peace with God through our Lord Jesus Christ,*
> *2 through whom we have gained access by faith into this grace in which we now stand. And we boast in the hope of the glory of God.*
> *3 Not only so, but we also glory in our sufferings, because we know that suffering produces perseverance;*
> *4 perseverance, character; and character, hope.*
> *5 And hope does not put us to shame, because God's love has been poured out into*

our hearts through the Holy Spirit, who has been given to us.

Romans 5:1-5

Now, the word used here for "perseverance" is the exact same word translated elsewhere as "patience."

What Paul is declaring in this magnificent truth is that the struggles we go through in life can work a process in us that produces some amazing things in our life. If we will let God use our struggles in life to produce patience (or perseverance), that patience will develop character in us. And character develops hope.

Hope is one of my favorite words in the Bible. It literally means "confident anticipation." Confident anticipation of what? That God is in control and He will accomplish His purpose and plan – and we get to be a part of it!

Think about that.

If we try to be patient and endure in our own strength, all we develop is a case of the "whymies."

The whymies?

Yes, the whymies. "Why me?"

However, if we let God's strength handle the struggles of our life, He develops patience and character in us that produces hope or "confident anticipation." I can't think of a more successful way to live life.

"Joyful thanksgiving"

There are more than two hundred references to a thankful attitude in the Bible. It's pretty important to God.

When Marcia and I were raising our three boys we taught them to say "thank you" when receiving something. Most parents do that. It's a matter of being polite. And it's a good habit.

We would teach them to say "thank you" whenever they got something.

But how do you teach gratitude?

More than just simply saying "thanks," gratitude is a matter of the heart. That's why Paul, in Colossians 1:10-12, refers to "joyfully giving thanks" as one of the ways we please God.

So how do you get from the duty of thanksgiving to the joy of thanksgiving?

Psalm 100 is a psalm for giving thanks, and it gives us some insight about how to develop a grateful heart:

A Psalm for Giving Thanks

> *1 Shout for joy to the LORD, all the earth.*
> *2 Worship the LORD with gladness; come before him with joyful songs.*

3 Know that the LORD is God. It is he who made us, and we are his; we are his people, the sheep of his pasture.

4 Enter his gates with thanksgiving and his courts with praise; give thanks to him and praise his name.

5 For the LORD is good and his love endures forever; his faithfulness continues through all generations.

Psalm 100

True thankfulness comes from realizing who we are and what we have in the light of God's love.

Notice the psalmist's insight:

The LORD is God. As a result we must understand that He made us and we belong to Him. He has a place and a purpose for each of us. We are His people. He is our Shepherd, and a shepherd provides for his sheep. He meets their needs.

The LORD is great. Now it doesn't actually say those words but the implication is there. He has gates and courts – items from a king's palace. And, amazingly, we are invited in.

The LORD is good. The last sentence of this psalm (verse 5) refers to three characteristics of God.

First, He is good. Good is a word that includes the concepts of graciousness, kindness, and generosity. God offers all of that to His own.

Secondly, He is loving. In fact, *"His love en-dures forever."* The word used here is actually a description of what love is like. It is a word that means kindness, mercy, and favor.

Thirdly, He is faithful. What an awesome thing to realize: your God is faithful. Even when you mess up and lose faith, He is faithful. Even when your life wobbles, He is steady. Even when you stumble, He is stable.

Now if God is all those things to you (and He is) and you begin to understand this amazing way God feels for you, you'll develop a gratitude that reach-es beyond the mundane circumstances of your life and seeks to acknowledge the ever-present passion that God has for you. That's thankfulness.

Thankfulness isn't just about appreciating the things you have. It goes way beyond that into the realm of overwhelming gratitude for who God is in your life, how He cares so deeply for you, and that He is more excited about His relationship with you than you are about Him.

Then something really special happens. You truly begin to trust God.

David, the psalmist, said it this way:

> *The LORD is my strength and my shield; my heart trusts in him, and I am helped. My heart leaps for joy and I will give thanks to him in song.*

> Psalm 28:7

When you finally trust God you begin to see Him lead you into His success.

"Share in the inheritance of the saints"

The final thing that Paul says in Colossians 1:10-12 is that God is apparently pleased for you *"to share in the inheritance of the saints in the kingdom of light."* In other words, God is pleased when you claim your godly inheritance!

We began this chapter as a follow-up to Paul's statement to the Corinthians:

> *So we make it our goal to please him, whether we are at home in the body or away from it.*
>
> 2 Corinthians 5:9

I made the statement that just as Paul's goal was to please God, so should each of us seek that same lofty goal. So how do you set and meet godly goals?

CHAPTER 5

YOUR GOAL – GOD'S WILL

Remember our definition of a goal: Accomplishing the intended result of a specific focus, strategy, and effort.

The only valid goals are ones *in the will of God.*

This may seem like an oversimplified and obvious truth, but far too many people miss this.

Since God created you and has a plan and purpose for your life, the only legitimate goals for you are those that are according to His will. Any goal that lies outside of His will—contrary to His plan for you—is a ticket to disaster.

Just as valid goals are those in the will of God, setting goals must take place within His will too. It makes no sense nor is it possible to set goals within God's will if you are not in His will when doing so.

It may seem that setting or meeting goals is nothing more than just doing God's will. While that may be an oversimplification, it is true. Your goals are simply the "how to" accomplish God's will.

Of course before you can discover "how to" accomplish God's will, you have to know His will. How is that possible? Well, here's some good news: God wants you to know His will far more than you do! He really does.

God isn't up in heaven saying "Guess what I want you to do next?" He wants you to know His will. Not only that, but He wants you to be sure that you know His will.

So how can you know God's will?

Believe that God wants you to know His will.

> *For it is God who works in you to will and to act according to his good purpose.*
>
> Philippians 2:13

This tends to be a self-worth issue. Too many people think that God's just not that interested in them, that He doesn't have a specific will for their lives. But that flies in the face of logic and truth.

God made you different from every other person in the world. Nobody ever has or ever will have the same characteristics, talents, and abilities that you possess, all rolled up into one body.

It will never happen again. Why did God make you that way?

He made you that way because He has a plan for your life. You are you by design!

If you are having trouble with this go back and read the part in chapter three about God's goals.

Understand how God reveals His will.

It seems the one thing Christians struggle with the most is knowing God's will. It is, of course, a most urgent issue for us. More importantly, it's an urgent issue for God. He wants us to know His will and accomplish it.

It's one of the reasons He gives us His Word.

> *I write these things to you who believe in the name of the Son of God so that you may know that you have eternal life.*
>
> 1 John 5:13

It's one of the reasons Jesus performed miracles.

> *But if I do it, even though you do not believe me, believe the works* [miracles], *that you may know and understand that the Father is in me, and I in the Father.*
>
> John 10:38(ESV)

God made you different from every other person in the world. Nobody ever has or ever will have the same characteristics, talents, and abilities that you possess, all rolled up into one body. It will never happen again. Why did God make you that way? He made you that way because He has a plan for your life. You are you by design!

It's even one of the reasons God allows us to go through trials and difficulties.

> ...*I did this so that you might know that I am the LORD your God.*
>
> Deuteronomy 29:6

Knowing God's will is one of the ultimate challenges for us. There are a number of ways that God reveals His will.

The first is through His Word. It is through God's Word that we find direction and discover truth.

> *Direct my footsteps according to your word; let no sin rule over me.*
>
> Psalm 119:133

Secondly, God reveals His will to our hearts.

> *Who endowed the heart with wisdom or gave understanding to the mind?*
>
> Job 38:36

Thirdly, even though we don't like to hear it, God speaks to us through crises to reveal His will. Sometimes, if we're not willing to get into His Word and discover His will, and we're not listening with our hearts, He has to use a crisis to get our attention. It happened with Elijah.

Elijah was so caught up in his own problems that he no longer really heard God. And God had to allow him to face a crisis to get his attention.

> *9 There he went into a cave and spent the night. And the word of the LORD came to him: "What are you doing here, Elijah?"*
> *10 He replied, "I have been very zealous for the LORD God Almighty. The Israelites have rejected your covenant, torn down your altars, and put your prophets to death with the sword. I am the only one left, and now they are trying to kill me too."*
> *11 The LORD said, "Go out and stand on the mountain in the presence of the LORD, for the LORD is about to pass by." Then a great and powerful wind tore the mountains apart and shattered the rocks before the LORD, but the LORD was not in the wind. After the wind there was an earthquake, but the LORD was not in the earthquake.*
> *12 After the earthquake came a fire, but the LORD was not in the fire. And after the fire came a gentle whisper.*
>
> 1 Kings 19:9-12

Sometimes we have to go through the storms and disasters of life to hear the whisper of God.

Know what God expects from you.

5 Trust in the LORD with all your heart and lean not on your own understanding; 6 in all your ways submit to him, and he will make your paths straight.

Proverbs 3:5-6

It's downright impossible to set goals if you don't know what God wants from your life.

Some things are pretty obvious. They are revealed in His Word. Those are the foundation for your life. That's why it is so important to spend time in God's Word. But the specific things are revealed through your personal relationship with God through focus, time, experience, and God's direction.

One of the comforting things to remember is that God really does want you to know His will. And because that is so important, it is His responsibility to make it clear to you.

However, sometimes God has to make some other things clear first.

When I went into the radio business I assumed that God wanted me in Christian broadcasting. Boy, was I wrong! I didn't even really get a chance to go down that path. I got fired sixty days to the day I was hired by a Christian broadcasting group because, as I was told, I didn't have what it took to be in radio.

I spent the next twenty-five-plus years on a secular radio morning show, and most of that time with top ratings.

My point is that God had to make it clear that He didn't intend for me to serve the next several years in Christian broadcasting. He was looking for me to serve Him as a Christian in secular broadcasting.

Sometimes God has to make some other things clear first, even if they seem like negatives or failures. So what is God trying to teach you right now?

Whatever God is teaching you right now is proof that God has plans for you. He has a goal for your life. Otherwise, why would He bother trying to mold you and shape you for what He wants to accomplish in and through your life?

So the question is, how do your goals compare to God's goals for your life?

No doubt everyone has goals. From the simple to the extravagant, we all have goals. I once asked a prisoner in a penitentiary what his goals were. He said, "Just to get through the day."

It is interesting that we equate a goal with winning. In fact, in some sports the whole purpose is to score a goal, and the team with the most goals wins. However, in life it's not quite the same simple process. An achieved goal is not the ultimate intent. Rather, a goal defines the blueprint for achieving success. That's why it is so critical to have the right goals.

During the last few days before His crucifixion, Jesus spent quite a bit of time preparing His disciples for their future. He told them what to expect and what would be expected of them. He gave them a foundation for the goals they would each need to implement in their life.

The most amazing thing that Jesus taught them was that He would send to them one who would direct their lives. He called Him the Comforter. We know Him as the Holy Spirit. It became very obvious that one of the key roles the Holy Spirit would play in their lives was to help them accomplish what God had in store for them. One of the main things the Holy Spirit would do is help them set and accomplish the goals that God had for them.

This is a supreme truth for the child of God. Reaching your goals must be rooted in the Holy Spirit.

> *5 Those who live according to the flesh have their minds set on what the flesh desires; but those who live in accordance with the Spirit have their minds set on what the Spirit desires.*

> *6 The mind governed by the flesh is death, but the mind governed by the Spirit is life and peace.*
>
> Romans 8:5-6

The apostle Paul asked:

> *Are you so foolish? After beginning by means of the Spirit, are you now trying to finish by means of the flesh?*
>
> Galatians 3:3

Paul was right. It just doesn't make sense.

The Holy Spirit plays such an integral part to your success – actually God's success through you.

Look at the following things that the Holy Spirit does. I've labeled each one according to the purpose of the Holy Spirit and given you a scriptural example:

1. Purpose of the Holy Spirit - Revelation

> *25 Now there was a man in Jerusalem called Simeon, who was righteous and devout. He was waiting for the consolation of Israel, and the Holy Spirit was on him.*
> *26 It had been revealed to him by the Holy Spirit that he would not die before he had seen the Lord's Messiah.*
>
> Luke 2:25-26

2. Purpose of the Holy Spirit - Motivation

Simeon was suddenly motivated by the Holy Spirit.

> *Moved by the Spirit, he went into the temple courts. When the parents brought in the child Jesus to do for him what the custom of the Law required....*
>
> Luke 2:27

Chapter nine will address Motivation in more detail.

3. Purpose of the Holy Spirit - Instruction

> *But the Counselor, the Holy Spirit, whom the Father will send in my name, will teach you all things and will remind you of everything I have said to you.*
>
> John 14:26

4. Purpose of the Holy Spirit - Conviction

> *7 But I tell you the truth: It is for your good that I am going away. Unless I go away, the Counselor will not come to you; but if I go, I will send him to you.*

8 When he comes, he will convict the world of guilt in regard to sin and righteousness and judgment.

John 16:7-8

5. Purpose of the Holy Spirit - Direction

But when he, the Spirit of truth, comes, he will guide you into all truth. He will not speak on his own; he will speak only what he hears, and he will tell you what is yet to come.

John 16:13

With all that the Holy Spirit is responsible for in your life, not to follow His direction is "foolish," as Paul pointed out in Galatians 3:3.

In fact, later in his letter to the Galatians Paul is even more emphatic about the need to follow the leading of the Holy Spirit:

The one who sows to please his sinful na-ture, from that nature will reap destruc-tion; the one who sows to please the Spirit, from the Spirit will reap eternal life.

Galatians 6:8

CHAPTER 6
THE POWER OF A PROMISE

This is one of my favorite chapters in this book. Please carefully read and ponder this.

Some of the biggest conflicts in our lives arise from our desire to live true to God's desire and will for our lives, yet facing the realities of every-day living. How can you be spiritual when you can't figure out which bills to pay and which to let slide? How can you be spiritual when you've got someone mouthing off at you? How can you be spiritual when you know things at work aren't what they're supposed to be?

One of the reasons we become so conflicted in life is because we haven't learned and believed that God's ways really are best for us. It's pretty easy to be faithful and spiritual when things are go-ing well in life, but what about when things don't go right? Is it possible to live the realities of life and still be right with God? Is it possible to know God's will and set constructive goals for life when we are surrounded by chaos and uncertainty?

The answer is yes!

So much so that God's promises prove that they are His will. God's promises give us the guidelines for our lives. Following God's promises; setting them as goals in our life, learning to apply them in our lives and obeying what the promises require of us will produce a radical change in life.

I want to share something with you that changed my life:

GOD'S PROMISES ARE THE REVELATION OF HIS WILL!

I had a discussion with a Christian who was having some real doubts. He wasn't even sure God existed. His words were, "I've never seen a God thing in my life."

I answered, "I presume you're not living in God's will?"

He went off on me. "God's will? How can you even know God's will? If God wants me to do His will, why does He make me guess what it is? If it's that big of a deal, shouldn't He make it very clear?"

Yes, He should, And He does! They're called promises.

If you don't know and apply God's promises, you aren't living in God's will. If you're not living in God's will, you're not enjoying the blessings of God. And if you're not applying the blessings of God, God is not real to you.

GOD'S PROMISES ARE THE REVELATION OF HIS WILL!

Even if you are a committed "church goer" and have been all your life. Even if you go through all the motions and emotions of Christianity, if you're not applying the promises of God, He isn't real to you. Oh, you may believe He's real, but He's not real in your life.

The fact is that applying God's promises is God's will for your life. One of the best ways to know God's will for your life is to know His promises.

God is a God of promises. There are thousands of promises in the Bible. Generally we consider around 3500 of them to be applicable for our lives, and the rest seem to be specific to people and events in the Bible. Herbert Lockyer wrote a book called All The Promises Of The Bible, and he lists over 8000 promises.

> *3 His divine power has given us everything we need for life and godliness through our knowledge of him who called us by his own glory and goodness.*
> *4 Through these he has given us his very great and precious promises, so that through them you may participate In the divine nature and escape the corruption in the world caused by evil desires.*
>
> 2 Peter 1:3-4

If it is important enough to God to make thousands of promises, it's important for us to discover why these promises are so important, and how to apply them in our lives. This is foundational to knowing God's will and setting goals for your life accordingly.

God's Promises Are An Affirmation Of His Intent.

God's promises are a window to His will. By knowing His promises we can know His desires. His promises reveal His intent and His plan.

Let me give you an example.

> *I will be a Father to you, and you will be my sons and daughters, says the Lord Almighty.*
> 2 Corinthians 6:18

Here we see God's intent to have a Father-child relationship with us. Think about that! God sees you as His child. He wants you to see Him as your Father. Now if you never had a good relationship with your earthly father this is difficult to understand and appreciate, but God wants the ideal Father-child relationship.

What is the ideal Father-child relationship? That's what God is looking for between you and Him.

In that simple promise we see one of God's goals for you and Himself. That opens up an incredible world of experiences. And believe me, that is even more exciting to God than it is to you! He longs for that kind of relationship and all that it has to offer.

God Acts On The Basis Of His Promises.

This was such an exciting realization for me.
God's promises tell us what God is up to! They
tell us how God thinks, how He acts and responds to the situations in our life. God doesn't
deviate from that. His promises are a roadmap to
what God is doing! We're taught that in the Old
Testament as well as the New Testament.

> *The Lord is faithful to all His promises...*
>   Psalm 145:13

> *...He who promised is faithful.*
>   Hebrews 10:23

If you'll take the time to study God's promises,
you'll begin to see how clearly God reveals Himself and His plans for your life!

God's Promises Are Based On His Purpose.

One of the greatest joys we have here on earth
as Christians is knowing that God has a purpose
and a will for each of us.

> *He has saved us and called us to a holy
> life--not because of anything we have done*

*but because of his own purpose and grace.
This grace was given us in Christ Jesus
before the beginning of time.*
2 Timothy 1:9

In other words, God has a purpose and will
for your life. Not because you're indispensable,
but because He wants to do something special
through you. Why does He want to do something
special through you? Noticed what I've under-
lined in these verses:

*5 [God] made us alive with Christ even
when we were dead in transgressions--it is
by grace you have been saved.
6 And God raised us up with Christ and
seated us with Him in the heavenly realms
in Christ Jesus,
7 in order that in the coming ages He might
show the incomparable riches of His grace, ex-
pressed in His kindness to us in Christ Jesus.*
Ephesians 2:5-7 (emphasis added)

*23 What if he did this to make the riches
of His glory known to the objects of His
mercy, whom He prepared in advance for
glory—
24 even us, whom He also called, not only
from the Jews but also from the Gentiles?*
Romans 9:23-24 (emphasis added)

God's will is revealed and supported through His promises. So, how can you apply God's promises?

Each promise comes with a unique set of benefits! But each benefit is also a discovery of how to discover and apply the promise. I call it:

The PromisePlus Principle

God's Promises Are Always Delivered In *His Presence.*

> *For no matter how many promises God has made, they are "Yes" in Christ. And so through him the "Amen" is spoken by us to the glory of God.*
>
> 2 Corinthians 1:20 (emphasis added)

This is critical to understand. According to this verse, all of God's promises to you are "in Christ" and "through Him". That means that to enjoy the full benefit of God's promises you have to have a right relationship and fellowship with Jesus Christ. A right relationship and fellowship with God will keep you in the presence of God where you can discover and enjoy His promises.

The relationship between God and Abraham is a great example of this. God said of Abraham:

> *For I have chosen him, so that he will di-*
> *rect his children and his household after*
> *him to keep the way of the LORD by doing*
> *what is right and just, so that the LORD*
> *will bring about for Abraham what he has*
> *promised him.*
>
> Genesis 18:19

Time and time again, God showed up in Abraham's life to reveal Himself and to deliver on His promise to him.

God's Promises Are Always Accomplished By *His Power*.

Abraham trusted the power of God. The apostle Paul said of Abraham:

> *20 Yet he did not waver through unbelief re-*
> *garding the promise of God, but was strength-*
> *ened in his faith and gave glory to God,*
> *21 being fully persuaded that God had*
> *power to do what he had promised.*
>
> Romans 4:20-21

God doesn't make promises that He can't deliver. God knows what He can do. When He made those promises for you in the Bible, He knew He had the power to make them happen in your life.

God's Promises Are Always Developed By *His Provision.*

Abraham didn't know how, when, or where, but he had to trust God would provide whatever was necessary to accomplish his plan and promises, even when it seemed completely implausible and impossible.

> *7 Isaac spoke up and said to his father Abraham, "Father?" "Yes, my son?" Abraham replied. "The fire and wood are here," Isaac said, "but where is the lamb for the burnt offering?"*
> *8 Abraham answered, "God himself will provide the lamb for the burnt offering, my son." And the two of them went on together...*
> *13 Abraham looked up and there in a thicket he saw a ram caught by its horns. He went over and took the ram and sacrificed it as a burnt offering instead of his son.*
> *14 So Abraham called that place The LORD Will Provide. And to this day it is said, "On the mountain of the LORD it will be provided."*
>
> Genesis 22:7-8,13-14

When you do His will you receive His promises... including His provision!

You need to persevere so that when you have done the will of God, you will receive what he has promised.

Hebrews 10:36

God's Promises Are Always Kept True By *His Protection.*

The promise to Abraham was never in doubt as far as God was concerned.

10 Then he reached out his hand and took the knife to slay his son.
11 But the angel of the LORD called out to him from heaven, "Abraham! Abraham!" "Here I am," he replied.
12 "Do not lay a hand on the boy," he said. "Do not do anything to him. Now I know that you fear God, because you have not withheld from me your son, your only son."

Genesis 22:10-12

God was testing Abraham's faithfulness to God over the promise.

This is important to note. God's promises reveal his will, but God is far more interested in our faithful fellowship with Him. So here's a question. Are you more interested in knowing God, or knowing what He can do for you?

19 O LORD. For the sake of your servant and according to your will, you have done this great thing and made known all these great promises.
20 "There is no one like you, O LORD, and there is no God but you, as we have heard with our own ears.

1 Chronicles 17:19-20

After Abraham proved his commitment to God, notice God's response:

15 The angel of the LORD called to Abraham from heaven a second time
16 and said, "I swear by myself, declares the LORD, that because you have done this and have not withheld your son, your only son,
17 I will surely bless you and make your descendants as numerous as the stars in the sky and as the sand on the seashore. Your descendants will take possession of the cities of their enemies,
18 and through your offspring all nations on earth will be blessed, because you have obeyed me."

Genesis 22:15-18

So...God's promises reveal His will. His promises are so remarkable! He is worthy of your commitment to Him!

Therefore, since we have these promises, dear friends, let us purify ourselves from everything that contaminates body and spirit, perfecting holiness out of reverence for God.

2 Corinthians 7:1

You may have heard the term "claim a promise." What does that mean?

When my children were small sometimes I would make promises to them like, "When I get home from work, I'll take you fishing." When got home that afternoon, the kids were waiting for me at the door, clamoring to go fishing. I'd made the promise and they were claiming it!

Imagine how disappointed I would have been if I had made the promise to take the kids fishing, and having planned on it, hurried home to spend that time with my children only to find that the kids had forgotten about the promise and were interested and involved in other things that didn't include me. That's how God must feel when His children ignore His promises.

Take inventory right now. How many of God's promises have you taken Him up on?

If you are having trouble knowing God's will for your life perhaps it's because you haven't discovered the obvious: God's promises reveal His will! By claiming His promises you are doing His will.

How many of God's promises have you taken Him up on?

God will honor <u>every</u> promise He has made.

Your kingdom is an everlasting kingdom, and your dominion endures through all generations. The LORD is faithful to all his promises and loving toward all he has made.
Psalm 145:13

What a remarkable statement! God's promises are not made frivolously. When God makes a promise, you can bet that it is something that God is planning to accomplish. Remember, a promise is the revelation of His will. A promise is a goal that God puts into action.

God is not human, that he should lie, not a human being, that he should change his mind. Does he speak and then not act? Does he promise and not fulfill?
Numbers 23:19

Claiming a promise is an act of faith.

14 For if those who live by law are heirs, faith has no value and the promise is worthless...
16 Therefore, the promise comes by faith...
Romans 4:14,16

In Chapter One we defined faith as "trusting obedience to the <u>known</u> will of God." Well, claiming a promise is simply obeying the known terms of the promise. For example:

> *...If you seek him, he will be found by you...*
> 1 Chronicles 28:9

Here is a promise that God will reveal Himself to those who seek Him. Note the terms and the promises in these verses:

> *14 Because he loves me," says the LORD, "I will rescue him; I will protect him, for he acknowledges my name.*
> *15 He will call upon me, and I will answer him; I will be with him in trouble, I will deliver him and honor him.*
> Psalm 91:14-15

Failing to claim the promises of God is actually sin.

> *24 Then they despised the pleasant land; they did not believe his promise.*
> *25 They grumbled in their tents and did not obey the LORD.*
> Psalm 106:24-25

Oh that we would be able to say as did Joshua at the end of his life:

> *Now I am about to go the way of all the earth. You know with all your heart and soul that not one of all the good promises the LORD your God gave you has failed. Every promise has been fulfilled; not one has failed.*

Joshua 23:14

CHAPTER 7
MAKE YOUR WORK EXTRAORDINARY

From the very beginning, God intended man to work:

> *The LORD God took the man and put him in the Garden of Eden to work it and take care of it.*
>
> Genesis 2:15

Think about it. Even in a perfect world, man and woman had to work. That was God's design.

Even Jesus had to work. Jesus was no pale weakling but a working man whose hands had been hardened by years of handling an ax, a saw, and a hammer. In fact, it would be safe to assume that Jesus put in a good fifteen years of carpentry work before He started His three and a half years of ministry. Hard physical labor was not beneath the dignity of the Son of God.

We are taught in the Bible to be good laborers and to manage our affairs well. In fact, I believe that every family unit, whether you're single, a couple, or a family with kids, should have a second business that they are developing. It's just a wise thing to do. And if you do have children, get them involved in it. What a great way to teach them the value of hard work and the joy of a job well done.

So if work is ordained by God, what's the reason for it?

God intends for people to be self-supporting. This principle is very clear in His Word.

> *You will eat the fruit of your labor; blessings and prosperity will be yours.*
>
> Psalm 128:2

> *11 ...make it your ambition to lead a quiet life: You should mind your own business and work with your hands, just as we told you,*
> *12 so that your daily life may win the respect of outsiders and so that you will not be dependent on anybody.*
>
> 1 Thessalonians 4:11-12

God also intends that people should find self-fulfillment in work.

> *All hard work brings a profit, but mere talk leads only to poverty.*
>
> Proverbs 14:23

This is a critical principle. The whole purpose of job-related work is to bring profit. Job-related work that doesn't bring profit isn't good enough. It may be noble, kind, philanthropic, and compassionate, but a job is about creating personal profit. Not just financial profit, but lifestyle profit.

18 This is what I have observed to be good: that it is appropriate for a person to eat, to drink and to find satisfaction in their toilsome labor under the sun during the few days of life God has given them—for this is their lot.
19 Moreover, when God gives someone wealth and possessions, and the ability to enjoy them, to accept their lot and be happy in their toil—this is a gift of God.
20 They seldom reflect on the days of their life, because God keeps them occupied with gladness of heart.

Ecclesiastes 5:18-20

God intends that work should enable us to serve others. This is a very important thing to understand. How does your job make it possible to serve others? Are you serving others, or just taking advantage of them? Are you making a positive difference in other people's lives?

Anyone who has been stealing must steal no longer, but must work, doing something

useful with their own hands, that they may have something to share with those in need.
Ephesians 4:28

15 She gets up while it is still night; she provides food for her family and portions for her female servants.
16 She considers a field and buys it; out of her earnings she plants a vineyard.
17 She sets about her work vigorously; her arms are strong for her tasks.
18 She sees that her trading is profitable, and her lamp does not go out at night.
Proverbs 31:15-18

Anyone who does not provide for their relatives, and especially for their own household, has denied the faith and is worse than an unbeliever.
1 Timothy 5:8

Above all, work should glorify God.

And whatever you do, whether in word or deed, do it all in the name of the Lord Jesus, giving thanks to God the Father through him.
Colossians 3:17

This can be a life-changing principle. Your work, your job, should be stimulated by your faith. In other words, your commitment to God is what motivates you to do what you do, including your job.

Far too many people spend their workdays doing what they have to do so they can do what they want to do, which is usually something that does not involve work. However, God says that we are to be challenged to do our jobs out of thanksgiving and obedience to Him.

> *5 Slaves, obey your earthly masters with respect and fear, and with sincerity of heart, just as you would obey Christ.*
> *6 Obey them not only to win their favor when their eye is on you, but as slaves of Christ, doing the will of God from your heart.*
> *7 Serve wholeheartedly, as if you were serving the Lord, not people,*
> *8 because you know that the Lord will reward each one for whatever good they do, whether they are slave or free.*
> *9 And masters, treat your slaves in the same way. Do not threaten them, since you know that he who is both their Master and yours is in heaven, and there is no favoritism with him.*
>
> Ephesians 6:5-9

Any legitimate work may be seen as God's calling if God enables you to have the job.

> *1 Then the LORD said to Moses,*
> *2 "See, I have chosen Bezalel son of Uri, the son of Hur, of the tribe of Judah,*

3 and I have filled him with the Spirit of God, with wisdom, with understanding, with knowledge and with all kinds of skills —
4 to make artistic designs for work in gold, silver and bronze,
5 to cut and set stones, to work in wood, and to engage in all kinds of crafts.
6 Moreover, I have appointed Oholiab son of Ahisamak, of the tribe of Dan, to help him. Also I have given ability to all the skilled workers to make everything I have commanded you.

Exodus 31:1-6

One of the amazing things that God does is call people to their ministry through their work.

70 He chose David his servant and took him from the sheep pens;
71 from tending the sheep he brought him to be the shepherd of his people Jacob, of Israel his inheritance.

Psalm 78:70-71

18 As Jesus was walking beside the Sea of Galilee, he saw two brothers, Simon called Peter and his brother Andrew. They were casting a net into the lake, for they were fishermen.
19 "Come, follow me," Jesus said, "and I will send you out to fish for people."

Matthew 4:18-19

Work will continue in the life to come. I don't know where the idea originated that we're going to spend eternity lying around popping grapes and playing harps. There will be work to do for eternity.

> *No longer will there be any curse. The throne of God and of the Lamb will be in the city, and his servants will serve him.*
>
> Revelation 22:3

Since *"his servants will serve him"* that obviously means we will have work to do.

It's hard to wrap our human minds around this, but think about this: all that God created was for a purpose.

> *The LORD has made everything for its purpose….*
>
> Proverbs 16:4

Now, if God created the incredible vastness of space, and everything He created has a purpose, and we will be serving Him for eternity, imagine the possibilities of what God might have in store for us! And if God has such amazing things in store for us, doesn't it make sense that what *we* are doing now—what we are going through here on earth—is part of the preparation for what God is planning?

If God created the incredible vastness of space, and every-thing He created has a purpose, and we will be serving Him for eternity, imagine the possibilities of what God might have in store for us!

I brought this up in a seminar I was teaching, and after the session a young man came to me and said, "Oh! I get it. Life on earth is like school before you get into the real world!"

So how can you make your work extraordinary? What can you do to become exceptional at work?

In the following passage Jesus is teaching about preparing for the end times, but within the context of the story we find some nuggets of right and wrong employer/employee actions, and some wonderful insight based on the cultural norms for work.

> *14 "Again, it will be like a man going on a journey, who called his servants and entrusted his wealth to them.*
>
> *15 To one he gave five bags of gold, to another two bags, and to another one bag, each according to his ability. Then he went on his journey.*
>
> *16 The man who had received five bags of gold went at once and put his money to work and gained five bags more.*
>
> *17 So also, the one with two bags of gold gained two more.*
>
> *18 But the man who had received one bag went off, dug a hole in the ground and hid his master's money.*

19 "After a long time the master of those servants returned and settled accounts with them.

20 The man who had received five bags of gold brought the other five. 'Master,' he said, 'you entrusted me with five bags of gold. See, I have gained five more.'

21 "His master replied, 'Well done, good and faithful servant! You have been faithful with a few things; I will put you in charge of many things. Come and share your master's happiness!'

22 "The man with two bags of gold also came. 'Master,' he said, 'you entrusted me with two bags of gold; see, I have gained two more.'

23 "His master replied, 'Well done, good and faithful servant! You have been faithful with a few things; I will put you in charge of many things. Come and share your master's happiness!'

24 "Then the man who had received one bag of gold came. 'Master,' he said, 'I knew that you are a hard man, harvesting where you have not sown and gathering where you have not scattered seed.

25 So I was afraid and went out and hid your gold in the ground. See, here is what belongs to you.'

26 "His master replied, 'You wicked, lazy servant! So you knew that I harvest where I have not sown and gather where I have not scattered seed?

27 Well then, you should have put my money on deposit with the bankers, so that when I returned I would have received it back with interest.

28 " 'So take the bag of gold from him and give it to the one who has ten bags.

29 For whoever has will be given more, and they will have an abundance. Whoever does not have, even what they have will be taken from them.

30 And throw that worthless servant outside, into the darkness, where there will be weeping and gnashing of teeth.'"

Matthew 25:14-30

We can discover from this passage six things that define a good employee.

1. First of all, verse 14 tells us that a good employee can be trusted with the employer's assets.

A company owner once shared with me how critical this issue is. He said, "I watch to see how an employee treats company property. I've learned that the ones who mishandle equipment they don't own mishandle their personal lives also, and that is an important factor for moving up the ladder in this business. The ones that take care of company equipment tend to be better at handling personal issues, and through the years I've noticed that they make better managers."

2. Verse 15 teaches us that a good employee works within his/her abilities – not less and not more.

Within this principle are some vital elements. A good employee will make his/her abilities clear to the employer. This isn't about showing off or seeking favoritism. It is about clarity.

Your employer needs to know what your abilities are. Not just what you think your abilities are, but what they really are because you've proved it.

I had a boss one time who kept a little placard in his office. It was placed on the front of his desk so that anyone sitting in the chair opposite him could see it. It read: "Don't tell me how good you are. Show me."

Another key element within this principle is that a good employee understands his/her value to the company. An employee will never spend more of themselves than they think they are worth. It's true in life and it is certainly true in the workplace.

One more key element in this principle is that a good employee understands where he/she fits into the order of responsibilities.

A manager once told me, "I need employees who are better at their own jobs than they are at mine."

3. Verse 16 tells us that a good employee responds immediately to tasks. That doesn't mean the job gets done immediately. Sometimes the task is a long project, but responding immediately to the assignment shows a healthy sense of responsibility and right priorities.

4. In verse 20 we see that a good employee is ready to give account for his/her accomplishments for the company. Again, this is not about showing off or seeking favoritism. This is about accountability.

If an employee or team of employees has been given an assignment, the good employee will be ready to explain what, how, and why they accomplished it—or have not accomplished it, which leads us to the next principle.

5. Verses 24-27 are a picture of a bad employee's actions. From that we can learn that:

A good employee assumes responsibility for his own actions.

A good employee does not blame others for his/her failure.

A good employee does not operate out of fear. This is important. Employees who operate out of fear make bad decisions, both at work and in their personal lives. Fear never leads to success. It almost always leads to failure.

A good employee does not make excuses for inadequacy. A bad employee will flounder in their inadequacies. A good employee will rise above their inadequacies by operating within their strengths.

6. Finally, a good employee is a problem solver.

I once had an outstanding office assistant. One of the things that made her so good was that she knew what her strengths and weaknesses were. She understood that when I asked her to do something, I wasn't telling her to do the job, I was assigning her the responsibility to get the job done. If she could handle the job, she did it. If she wasn't able to handle the job, she knew how to find a way to get the job done. She was a problem solver.

Using that same passage in Matthew 25, we can also discover what makes a good employer. Verses 14 and 15 tell us that:

A good employer knows his employees.

He knows their abilities.

He knows what he can trust them with.

One must presume that in order to know his employees, he has to spend time with them on the job.

It's interesting to note that from the very onset of this story we know the one-talent guy is going to mess up. His employer doesn't trust him enough to give him more responsibility. Why? More than likely because of past experience.

Verse 19 reminds us that a good employer holds his employees accountable.

This is not only good for productivity, it's good for morale. Employees need to know that they are accountable. They also need to know that when a coworker is not pulling his weight, he's going to be held accountable. One of the biggest complaints in the workplace is that slackers aren't held accountable.

Verses 20-23 tell us that a good employer rewards good employees.

A friend once told me about his work situation. Apparently it was a miserable place to work. His boss was a tyrant, so much so that he wouldn't allow any kind of award or reward. He actually told the employees, "Your reward is you get to keep your job."

My friend remarked that every time the boss said that he thought to himself *that's not a reward; that's a sentence.*

Good employers reward good employees. Whether it be with promotions or awards or time off, or something to add to a pleasing work environment, good employers value their employees. Why?

It goes back to something mentioned earlier about good employees. An employee will spend as much of himself as he thinks he's worth to the company. An employer who doesn't value his employees isn't going to get any more out of them than the way he treats them.

Verse 27 teaches us that a good employer makes his/her expectations very clear.

Some time ago I led a Success Strategy Seminar for an overseas company. Before the seminar, as I often do, I spent a couple of days just hanging out in the various company departments, getting a feel for the attitude and work environment. There was one department that I couldn't figure out. I asked one of the employees I had befriended in that department what they did.

He laughed and said, "We're the Guessing Department. We have to guess what our boss wants us to do!"

It turns out the boss really did have very little communication with this department. He would post memos on the bulletin board or tell one of the employees to pass on a directive. Aside from that, about the only time they would see him was when something had gone wrong.

Finally, verse 30 tells us that a good employer doesn't put up with bad employees.

One of the biggest mistakes a company makes is keeping employees that do not produce value for the company. Bad employees are a drain on the company's assets. The bottom line is that good employees make profits and bad employees cut into profits.

Not only that, but bad employees are counterproductive to the success of the other employees.

Because the worthless employee in the Matthew passage produced no value, he in essence kept the other employees from producing even greater value. Those employees were not able to use the designated assets of the worthless employee, and so they were not able to produce greater value. Not only did he hold the company back, he also held the other employees back. That wasn't fair to the company or the other employees.

But here's what some companies are doing: since cash flow and profit margins are critical to company value, some companies keep the worthless employee because they don't have to pay him very much and get rid of the first employee, who produced so much. Why? Because they have to pay him more and that cuts into cash flow and current profit margins.

If they can get rid of him and lean on the second employee to pick up his productivity, they think they'll have better cash flow and higher profit margins. The problem with this scenario is that while it may look good on paper, and may put more immediate money in the owner's pockets, it is a failure spiral that will eventually catch up to the company. Of course by then upper management hopes they'll be out of the picture and won't have to worry about it.

So the high producer gets canned. The worthless employee stays. And the pressure is piled on the second employee to operate beyond his abilities, putting him under tremendous stress and making his life miserable.

That's not productive management. And it runs completely counter to the biblical examples of good management. A company is far better off by getting rid of the employees who are a drag on the productivity of the company or department, and rewarding the employees who are a value to the company. While the immediate loss of staff may be a burden, in the long run, the company is better off, and the good employees are happier, and more productive.

If you want to learn how to be a great manager, a great employer, study the life of Moses or Nehemiah. Discover how they handled people and conflict. Observe their great management decisions.

I mentioned earlier about leading a Success Strategy Seminar. I had the privilege of leading several of those seminars in the Philippines a few years ago.

One of the basic principles I taught was that if companies will help their employees become personally successful, those employees will by default make the company successful. It just makes sense. If I use my company to make my employees successful (instead of using the employees to make me successful), the process of making them successful makes my company successful. It's a biblical principle:

Give, and it will be given to you. A good measure, pressed down, shaken together and running over, will be poured into your lap. For with the measure you use, it will be measured to you.

Luke 6:38

The next year, when I went back, I spoke to the combined Rotary clubs of Manila. The president of the host club introduced me before I spoke. He said, "Last year I went to one of these seminars. I thought it couldn't hurt. Our company was struggling and we needed some direction. I went back to work the very next week and changed our whole company philosophy concerning our employees. I decided that we would focus on making our employees personally successful. I gathered our employees together and asked them to design plans that would make them successful by using the company. It completely turned the company around. In one year, our business went up by 20 percent, and not one employee left us. And now I have a huge stack of job applications from people wanting to work for us."

Your job can be extraordinary when you fulfill God's plan for your work. What is He up to in you and through you where you work?

What does He want to accomplish through you to impact where you work?

Every day you have a job is an opportunity to glorify God. Every day you have a job is an opportunity to fulfill His purpose and plan in and through your life.

But remember God's goals can never be reached in human efforts or terms. No matter how sincere you are or how hard you work, you will never achieve God's goals for you in your own strength and effort.

Reaching godly goals must be accomplished in a godly manner. That's why you need the leadership and power of the Holy Spirit to achieve your goals. You simply cannot succeed any other way.

> *May he give you the desire of your heart and make all your plans succeed.*
> Psalm 20:4

CHAPTER 8

THE SECRET TO
FINANCIAL SUCCESS

Got your attention didn't I? For some reason we think there is a secret to financial success. That's why I titled this chapter that way. Actually it's not completely misleading. Apparently not many people have discovered this wonderful truth you're about to learn. So I guess it's still sort of a secret. That's a shame.

We humans equate financial gain with success, but God doesn't see it that way. Not that there may not be some financial gain attached to the success God offers. However, His kind of financial success is very different from the world's success.

In this chapter we will address personal finances. That's because our business finances tend to follow our personal finance habits. Get your personal finances straightened out and in doing so you'll discover the necessary principles for your business finances, and vice versa. One of the companies that I do some work for operates this way. The company is totally debt free, and they encourage their people to live their lives that way. In fact, they even have some plans and training to help their people get out of debt. It's a remarkable, rewarding challenge.

One of the biggest problems that Christians deal with is finances. We struggle to balance our commitment to Christ with our earthly responsibilities. We have desires to improve our lot in life, to provide for our families, to plan for the future, and to enjoy life through the conveniences and pleasures that money can buy. Add to that conflict a sense of obligation to the local church and you've got the makings of financial chaos.

This is especially true for young couples planning or starting a family. Some of the biggest decisions about life are often made at a time when one isn't quite ready emotionally, socially, or financially to make such decisions. Young couples often make dangerous financial choices early in their marriages that affect them negatively for many years; choices about a home, cars, furniture, babies, and jobs. Some of the biggest financial commitments are made when the couple is at the lower end of their earning power. Seems unfair doesn't it?

And if two people who have each made unwise financial choices fall in love and get married, they usually compound their financial dilemma. Their marriage is already in trouble *before* they get married because of the wrong financial choices they have made.

Then there are the median to older adults who are reaping the consequences of financial choices they made earlier in life. And if their bad choices are complicated by difficult circumstances such as medical problems or an unstable economy, they find themselves in a frightening situation. It becomes even worse if they have to depend on adult children who are already in financial difficulties.

Does the Bible have anything to say about personal finances? Absolutely! In fact, the Bible has a lot to say about your finances. The same God who wants you to be free from the burden of your sin, free from worry, and free from satanic oppression also wants you to be free from financial depression. Not that He wants you to be wealthy from the world's standpoint. The Bible doesn't teach that. But God does want you to be free from financial bondage.

The fact is that God desires you to be free from *all* bondage in your life. He is a God who knows that living in bondage, particularly financial bondage, is counterproductive. People in financial bondage cannot enjoy life to the fullest. But Jesus said that His intent was to give us *"life to the fullest"* (John 10:10).

The same God who wants you to be free from the burden of your sin, free from worry, and free from satanic oppression also wants you to be free from financial depression.

Take a look at what God says about His desire for you to be free from bondage, including financial difficulties:

> *7 He upholds the cause of the oppressed and gives food to the hungry. The LORD sets prisoners free,*
> *8 the LORD gives sight to the blind, the LORD lifts up those who are bowed down, the LORD loves the righteous.*
>   Psalm 146:7-8

> *It is for freedom that Christ has set us free. Stand firm, then, and do not let yourselves be burdened again by the yoke of slavery.*
>   Galatians 5:1

But in that same chapter of Galatians, Paul points out that with freedom comes responsibility:

> *You, my brothers, were called to be free. But do not use your freedom to indulge the sinful nature....*
>   Galatians 5:13

To understand how God wants to free you financially, you need to know how and why you may be in financial straits. It usually boils down to three things:

1. Not believing that God has your best interests at heart.
2. Not trusting God as your source.
3. Mismanagement of what God has given
   you.

Let's look at each of these.

Not believing that God has your best interests at heart.

This is a simple problem with severe consequences. It is the result of not having an intimate relation-ship with God, and therefore not trusting Him. As we go through life, getting deceived and taken ad-vantage of, we learn to mistrust others. We come to believe the only person we can trust is ourself. That carries over into our relationship with God.

That's similar to what happened with Adam and Eve as described in Genesis.

> *1 Now the serpent was more crafty than any of the wild animals the LORD God had made. He said to the woman, "Did God really say, 'You must not eat from any tree in the garden'?"*
> *2 The woman said to the serpent, "We may eat fruit from the trees in the garden,*

3 but God did say, 'You must not eat fruit from the tree that is in the middle of the garden, and you must not touch it, or you will die.' "

4 "You will not certainly die," the serpent said to the woman.

5 "For God knows that when you eat from it your eyes will be opened, and you will be like God, knowing good and evil."

6 When the woman saw that the fruit of the tree was good for food and pleasing to the eye, and also desirable for gaining wisdom, she took some and ate it. She also gave some to her husband, who was with her, and he ate it.

7 Then the eyes of both of them were opened, and they realized they were naked; so they sewed fig leaves together and made coverings for themselves.

8 Then the man and his wife heard the sound of the LORD God as he was walking in the garden in the cool of the day, and they hid from the LORD God among the trees of the garden.

9 But the LORD God called to the man, "Where are you?"

10 He answered, "I heard you in the garden, and I was afraid because I was naked; so I hid."

> *11 And he said, "Who told you that you
> were naked? Have you eaten from the tree
> that I commanded you not to eat from?"*
> *12 The man said, "The woman you put here
> with me —she gave me some fruit from the
> tree, and I ate it."*
> *13 Then the LORD God said to the woman,
> "What is this you have done?" The woman
> said, "The serpent deceived me, and I ate."*
> Genesis 3:1-13

Satan put a seed of doubt in their minds about God's intentions and reasons for forbidding them to eat from the tree of the knowledge of good and evil. In fact, he deceptively asked, *"Did God really say, 'You must not eat from any tree in the garden?'* (Genesis 3:1).

That seed of doubt developed into mistrust and misinterpretation of what God actually said. Eve twisted what God said (v. 3), and Satan (the serpent) brought that grain of doubt into full-blown mistrust when he told her, *"You will not surely die...for God knows that when you eat of it your eyes will be opened, and you will be like God, knowing good and evil"* (Genesis 3:4-5).

In the very next verse we read how Eve's mistrust of God led to her disobedience.

The same thing happens today. People mistrust God. They don't believe that He has their best interests at heart, and they decide they will have to take care of themselves. The result is basically the same thing that happened to Adam and Eve: fellowship with God is broken, plunging man into a dismal darkness in which he wanders around trying to fend for himself, ignoring God's purpose and plan, and messing up his life at every turn.

The fact is that God does have our best interests at heart. He proved it through Jesus Christ.

> *But God demonstrates His own love for us in this: While we were still sinners, Christ died for us.*
>
> Romans 5:8

There is nothing greater God could have done to prove that He cares about us and that we are of ultimate importance to Him.

Not trusting God as your source.

If we don't believe that God has our best interests at heart, the next step becomes one of mistrusting God as our resource. We simply don't believe that God is our provider—our source. That dangerous step leads us to depend on ourselves. When we do that, we begin ignoring God's plan for our lives and start making our own choices and decisions without regard to God's desires.

God never intended man to plot and plan his own life. The reason is very simple. God explained it this way through Jeremiah:

> *5 ...Cursed is the one who trusts in man, who draws strength from mere flesh and whose heart turns away from the LORD.*
> *6 That person will be like a bush in the wastelands; they will not see prosperity when it comes....*
>
> Jeremiah 17:5-6

And later in verse 9 God says:

> *The heart is deceitful above all things and beyond cure. Who can understand it?*
>
> Jeremiah 17:9

Because our sinful nature is to trust ourselves over God, which is sin, the end results are disastrous.

> *Woe to those who plan iniquity, to those who plot evil on their beds! At morning's light they carry it out because it is in their power to do it.*
>
> Micah 2:1

See the tailspin we get into when we mistrust God? What starts out perhaps as sin with minor consequences ends up as sin with major consequences. Micah goes on to explain that such people end up hurting others with little or no regard for their rights or circumstances.

Paul's letter to the Romans explains it this way:

> *Those who live according to the sinful nature have their minds set on what that nature desires....*
>
> Romans 8:5

Sin breeds sin. You deceive yourself if you believe that you can do something wrong for the right reasons. That is an act of desperation and proof that God is not your source. This is one reason why so many people have a problem with gambling.

If God is not your source you cut yourself off from the blessings He wants to pour out on you.

The fact is that God really does want to pour out blessings on your life! It has been my experience that He wants to bless us in abundance beyond the limitations of money.

God is in the business of meeting needs, but sin attacks needs and in reality creates greater needs. If you make financial decisions without regard to God's desires, and without trusting Him as your source, you will end up creating greater problems for yourself—the consequences of your sin.

Mismanagement of what God has given you.

If you don't believe that God has your best interests at heart, and you don't trust Him as your
source, the end result will be that you mismanage and misuse what God has provided for you.
Specifically, you will mismanage your money.
It stands to reason. If you aren't really seeking
God's will for your life, those areas in which you
have not given God control will control you to
your harm.

One of the most significant areas in which Christians mismanage their money is the tithe. This
subject causes an awful lot of debates and arguments. Excuses for not tithing are offered such
as: "That's an Old Testament thing" or "We're not
under the law anymore. We're under grace."

Yes, it is an "Old Testament thing." But it's a
New Testament thing also. Jesus referred to it,
and tithing was an active element of the New
Testament church, even after Christ died and
rose again. By the way, the tithe existed long before the law. Genesis 14:20 tells us that Abram
paid the tithe even before the law was passed
down through Moses. Jacob also committed himself to the tithe in Genesis 28. It's affirmed in the
New Testament in Hebrews 7:4.

The problem we have with the tithe is that we
don't understand what it's all about. We tend to

think of it as dues to the church, and we believe we need that money more than the church does. But the tithe is not ours. It doesn't even belong to the church.

The tithe belongs to God. It does not belong to you. It's not your money. It's God's. In Malachi 3, God accuses His people of stealing from Him because they kept the tithe.

Now, note that the tithe is different from an offering. The tithe is 10 percent of our income whereas an offering is an amount of our own choosing, or God's leading, over and above the tithe.

Why is the tithe such a big deal?

Two reasons. First, your obedience to God regarding the tithe releases Him to pour out blessings on you.

> *The best of all the firstfruits and of all your special gifts will belong to the priests. You are to give them the first portion of your ground meal so that blessing may rest on your household.*
>
> Ezekiel 44:30

> *Bring the whole tithe into the storehouse, that there may be food in my house. Test me in this," says the LORD Almighty,*

> *"and see if I will not throw open the flood-*
> *gates of heaven and pour out so much*
> *blessing that you will not have room*
> *enough for it.*
>
> Malachi 3:10

Secondly, the tithe is the way God supports His church throughout the world. It is the way God has chosen to fund His church ministries. He gives very specific instructions about it. It's that important! We are told to bring our tithes to our church for God's purposes.

Look at it this way: you are the courier of that money. God pays you 90 percent to deliver that 10 percent. God is trusting you to deliver that amount to His local church to be used for His kingdom. He is expecting you to deliver that 10 percent.

If I call a courier to deliver a package from my company to another, I expect that courier to do what I'm paying for. If along the way the courier looks in the package and decides he needs that item more than the company he's delivering it to, what has he done? He has stolen. Stolen from my company and stolen from the company to which he was to deliver the item.

That's exactly what you do when you fail to deliver the tithe. You steal from God. You prove to God that you are not trustworthy. So why should He entrust you with a greater amount to deliver? You see, God is your source, your provider. Your job is not your source. God is. God uses your job to deliver your income *and* the income for His church ministries. He gives you 90 percent and He uses that 10 percent for His purposes.

If you cannot be trusted to deliver the 10 percent, why should God increase your income? Why should He increase the amount the 90 percent represents if He can't trust you to do what you're supposed to do with the 10 percent?

It's a sure thing that if you are not managing the tithe correctly, you are not managing the rest of your budget correctly. And if you are not managing your budget correctly, you're either already in a mess or you're flirting with disaster.

So what is the secret to financial success? Here it is:

God's will done God's way will never lack for God's provision

This is one of the greatest principles that we can live by. When we do things God's way, He provides the resources. When we live our lives financially the way God wants us to, He will provide the finances He wants us to use.

God's will done God's way will never lack for God's provision

God is in the business of meeting needs. That's what He does.

He knows your needs. He knows how to meet your needs. However, He may decide to meet your needs in ways that you do not expect. The key is to trust that God has your best interests at heart, that He is your source, and that He will meet your needs.

That puts financial success in a whole different light, doesn't it?

Now some might say this approach to our finances suggests that we don't need to plan ahead, that we aren't supposed to save money and invest it wisely. Actually, we are to do just the opposite.

> *Dishonest money dwindles away, but he who gathers money little by little makes it grow.*
> Proverbs 13:11

But money isn't something that we are to hoard.

> *Whoever loves money never has money enough; whoever loves wealth is never satisfied with his income. This too is meaningless.*
> Ecclesiastes 5:10

The reason God treats money this way is because money is not something to own. God sees it as a tool, a way to accomplish His purposes and plans which include blessing you and others – although maybe not always in financial ways.

Read Genesis 47 and look at how God used Jacob to save the Egyptians from starvation. Their money wasn't enough to save them. But Jacob used their money and possessions, invested it wisely, and saved the land. He didn't take their money and land to hoard it. He apparently used it as a tool to buy food and grain and eventually bring wealth and stability back to the land.

Read Leviticus 25 and discover how money was never to be used to own a person or land permanently but rather as a tool to help people stabilize their lives.

In 2 Kings 12 and 2 Chronicles 24 we find the account of King Joash, a good king who was later assassinated by some of his officials. Joash was known for instructing the priests to collect offerings and a tax that Moses established and then use that money to hire the people to work on the temple. He didn't hoard the money, although the priests at first tried to do that. He used the money as a tool to accomplish God's purpose and plan.

Even the early church applied this principle:

> *34 There were no needy persons among them. For from time to time those who owned lands or houses sold them, brought the money from the sales*

35 and put it at the apostles' feet, and it was distributed to anyone as he had need.
Acts 4:34-35

So what is the bottom line?

Do it God's way. He is after all your source. Doesn't it make sense that the one who meets our need is the One who should determine how His supply is used and spent?

One of the greatest passages in the Bible is a doxology given to us by the apostle Paul in his letter to the Romans. Interestingly enough it's about this very subject:

33 Oh, the depth of the riches of the wisdom and knowledge of God! How unsearchable his judgments, and his paths beyond tracing out!

34 Who has known the mind of the Lord? Or who has been his counselor?

35 Who has ever given to God, that God should repay him?

36 For from him and through him and to him are all things. To him be the glory forever! Amen.
Romans 11:33-36

CHAPTER 9

MOTIVATED BY GOD

So how do you take all this and put it into play?

There is simply no better way to live your life than to do so within the boundaries that God has set for you, motivated by Him. And that's a key aspect to all of this – to be motivated. Not motivated by self. That's a dead-end disaster. But by the One who is our source and provider.

Yes! God really does motivate us. He has not left us to our own ways. He doesn't tell us to do something a particular way and then leave the rest up to us.

People often refer to me as a motivational speaker, but I hate that term. It's so condescending. It implies that my audience is lethargic and unproductive, and my job is to whip them into a frenzy to go out and change the world.

The truth of the matter is I have never motivated anyone. Never.

In the secular world, when I'm leading a conference, I define motivation this way:

Motivation: the desire, drive, and design to move from one comfort zone to another

There is nothing wrong with a comfort zone if it is the right place to be. However, motivation requires that once you recognize that the comfort zone you are in needs to change, you must be willing to change. To move from one comfort zone to another requires the desire to leave one defined way of life and move to another defined way of life. Along with that, you must have the drive to do what it takes to reach that new comfort zone. And finally, you must have a plan – a design in place to make the move.

That works in a secular and business sense. But for God's people, called for His purposes and plans, it makes no sense for us to have to motivate ourselves. After all, God has called us. Shouldn't He be the One who stimulates us to action?

When my boys were young, if I wanted them to do something I first had to make my wishes clear and then motivate them to do it. And no, I don't mean by threatening them. I mean reinforcing and encouraging them to get the job done. I would maybe offer a reward or promise some playtime. Or sometimes I would just let them know that their well-done job would please me.

Our heavenly Father works much the same way. Not only does He reveal His will to us but He also motivates us to accomplish it. Sometimes the motivation comes gently. Sometimes strongly. Sometimes there is the promise of a reward. And sometimes, because of rebellion or stubbornness on our part, He has to be firm or even harsh.

Read the story of Jonah. Now there was a guy who needed some godly motivation!

Interestingly, in the very first chapter we read that God used Jonah's rebellion and stubbornness as an example to some men on the ship Jonah was sailing on to get away from God. Now get this: Jonah's rebellion caused them to repent and get right with God!

> *At this the men greatly feared the LORD, and they offered a sacrifice to the LORD and made vows to him.*
>
> Jonah 1:16

Throughout the story we see a number of ways that God sought to motivate Jonah. First was the simple call:

> *Go to the great city of Nineveh and preach against it, because its wickedness has come up before me.*
>
> Jonah 1:2

Second was the storm at sea:

> *Then the LORD sent a great wind on the sea, and such a violent storm arose that the ship threatened to break up.*
>
> Jonah 1:4

Then there was that big fish:

> *But the LORD provided a great fish to swallow Jonah, and Jonah was inside the fish three days and three nights.*
>
> Jonah 1:17

And there was a second call:

> *Go to the great city of Nineveh and proclaim to it the message I give you.*
>
> Jonah 3:2

Finally, God accomplished His purpose in sending Jonah to Nineveh:

> *When God saw what they did and how they turned from their evil ways, he had compassion and did not bring upon them the destruction he had threatened.*
>
> Jonah 3:10

That irritated Jonah because he hated Nineveh. Let that be a lesson to you. Sometimes God calls you and motivates you to something you personally find unpleasant or unacceptable, even abhorrent.

The good news is that God's motivation doesn't have to come the way it did with Jonah. It did in Jonah's case because of his obstinate ways, but the motivation didn't have to be that way.

How does God prefer to motivate you?

It's found in a simple little verse in Psalm 37 that is often misunderstood and misquoted:

> *Delight yourself in the LORD and he will give you the desires of your heart.*
>
> Psalm 37:4

The word "delight" here means to be tender or to take pleasure in something. The idea is that you find your joy and pleasure in the Lord. It's very much a romantic term.

When I bring a gift to my wife, I watch her to see how she reacts. Is she pleased with the gift? Is it important to her? Is she pleased with me for giving it to her? That's the concept of this verse – to seek your joy in God, to seek to please Him.

When that happens, you free up God for the second part of the verse, and this is the part that is often misunderstood. This verse is not saying that if you "delight yourself in the Lord" He will give you whatever you want. That would lead us to try to manipulate God, and that never works!

Although the word for "desires" is the same word for requests or petitions, it doesn't mean such things come from personal want. In fact it says that they come because He puts those matters in your heart.

The verse is saying that when you "delight yourself in the Lord" He will put His desires in your heart! In other words He will begin to motivate you to do what He wants from you.

What an awesome and successful way to live your life: you finding pleasure in the Lord, and Him motivating you to do His will! Now that's what I call a working relationship!

The great thing about this truth is its simplicity. Your responsibility is not to motivate yourself but rather to focus on God and to "delight" in Him. It's His responsibility to motivate you.

What an amazing journey lies ahead of you!

Success—something that God planned for you millions of years ago. He knew you millions of years ago, and He has been planning your success ever since.

Let me quote a verse we looked at back in chapter three:

When you "delight yourself in the Lord" He will put His desires in your heart! In other words He will begin to motivate you to do what He wants from you.

> *For I know the plans I have for you,"* de-
> clares the LORD, *"plans to prosper you and
> not to harm you, plans to give you hope and
> a future.*
>
> Jeremiah 29:11

God has been planning your success and your future for a long time. If it's that important to God it should be that important to you.

And it is important to do it God's way!

Now start reading the book again. Read it several times. The more these principles and scriptures get in your head, the more they will start working in you to accomplish God's intent.

I pray that God has used this book to teach and inspire you. We've only covered some of the important basics. What you've seen here is just a grain of sand compared to the vastness of God's plan for your success. Every day as you walk in the Spirit, God will reveal new and exciting things to you. I believe that one of the greatest pleasures God has is revealing Himself to His children.

> *May he give you the desire of your heart
> and make all your plans succeed.*
>
> Psalm 20:4

FINAL THOUGHTS

Our world is crying out for successful people. The world is desperate for people to show them how to get the most out of life—how to succeed. Those of us who seek to live that personal relationship with God have a tremendous responsibility to be an example and do it God's way.

What will you do with the biblical principles set forth in this book?

I can tell you that in my business God has seen fit to provide success in the midst of one of the worst economic times of our nation.

You see, success isn't dependent on the economy. It's dependent on God's blessing.

We saw this verse back in the chapter on finances, but it's appropriate to close with this magnificent promise:

...test me in this," says the LORD Almighty, "and see if I will not throw open the flood-gates of heaven and pour out so much blessing that you will not have room enough for it.

Malachi 3:10

ABOUT THE AUTHOR

Dan Hurst is the lead teacher for The Open Class, a Bible study he started at First Baptist Church of Raytown, Missouri. The class has several hundred members.

As the son of missionary parents to Honduras, he grew up in a culture of ministry based on teaching God's Word in a way that can be understood practically and applied. Many of those principles carried over to his ministry efforts as a Bible teacher.

Dan and his wife, Marcia, live in the Kansas City area. Although his business, conference speaking, and teaching keep him busy, he finds time to ruin some golf courses and cheer on Kansas City's sports teams.

To contact Dan Hurst:

Living Power
Publishing

www.LivingPower.com
(660) 851–1510